First published 1972
Macdonald and Co
(Publishers) Limited
St Giles House
49–50 Poland Street
London W1

© Macdonald and Co
(Publishers) Limited 1972

Made by:
Morrison & Gibb Ltd
Edinburgh, Scotland

Managing Editor
Chris Milsome

Editor
Angela Littler

Illustrators
Patricia Lenander
Malcolm McGregor

Projects
John Taunton

Project Illustrators
Robert Gillmor
John Yates

Production
Stephen Pawley
Philip Hughes

Picture Research
Penny Warn
Jackie Newton

Sources of Photographs
The Zoological Society of London
The Nature Conservancy
Greenhill and Ellis

Series devised by
Peter Usborne

SBN 356 04095X

The Life of Birds

A simple introduction to bird behaviour for younger readers. Special reference and projects section

Macdonald
Educational

Dr. Maurice Burton

The Life of Birds

People have always been fascinated by birds, and a great many books have been written on the subject. Traditionally, most of these books aim to classify the different species of birds. This book has an entirely new approach.

The Life of Birds is an exciting visual study for young readers of the behaviour of birds. It traces their ancestry and evolution. It looks at the structure of their bodies, the way they fly, how they mate, how they defend themselves and their families, what they eat, and the way they communicate with each other. It highlights some of the more unusual facts discovered about birds, and deals with related topics in a new and interesting way.

Full colour illustrations are used wherever possible to emphasize aspects of bird life, such as the wonderful camouflage of plumage and eggs, the making of a nest, mating and hatching, the anatomy of a bird, and the way its body is adapted to flight. In dealing with subjects such as migration, the book not only shows where birds go, but also why they go, and how they find the way.

The last section of the book is a reference and project section full of information, and practical suggestions for enthusiastic readers to follow.

The Life of Birds is the first book in the *Macdonald Introduction to Nature* series. In line with the latest teaching methods, it explores its subject from as many viewpoints as possible, and incorporates many related topics.

Contents

Reference and Projects

How Birds Began

There have not always been birds on earth. It took a long time before the ancestors of today's birds appeared.

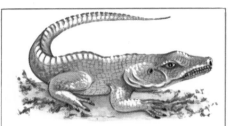

The first of all the reptiles looked like the lizards of today. They crawled around on all fours. Their back legs were only a little longer than their front legs.

Over a long period of time, some reptiles began to develop long back legs and short front legs. They could stand upright on their back legs. They were called bipedal, which means two-footed.

When the bipedal reptiles ran, they used their front legs to keep their balance. Some of them may have flapped their front legs, like tiny wings. They developed feathers instead of scales.

With the appearance of feathers, came the first birds. They probably took to the trees for shelter. They were not able to fly very well, and could perhaps only glide by jumping from trees.

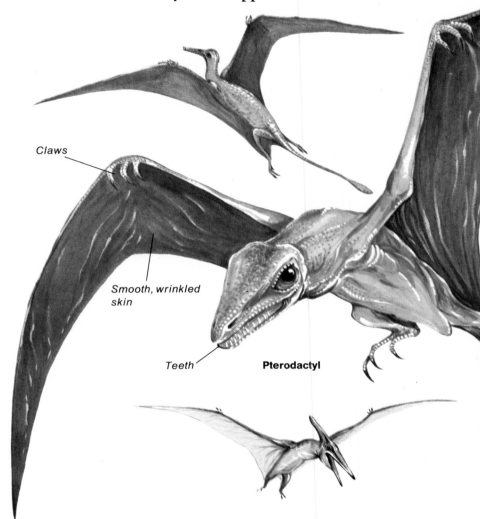

Claws

Smooth, wrinkled skin

Teeth

Pterodactyl

The First Birds

A very long time ago, the most common animals living on earth were reptiles. They had cold blood and were covered with scales. They crawled around on all fours. At that time, man had not yet appeared on earth.

Some of the early reptiles developed wings and feathers and learnt to fly. They were the first birds.

Pterodactyls

Other reptiles also took to the air. They were called pterodactyls (ter-o–dak-tils). Their wings were made of skin. They had no feathers and could only glide.

The pterodactyls died out. They did not become birds, since they did not develop feathers. The proof of their existence is found in fossils.

Fossils

Fossils are the remains of plants and animals of long ago found buried in rocks, or sometimes in ice or amber. A fossil has been found of what is probably the first bird. It is called the archaeopteryx (ar-ki-op-ter-iks).

Experts can find out many things from fossils. They can tell what the plants and animals of the past looked like. They can see what changes have taken place by comparing fossils with present–day animals and plants.

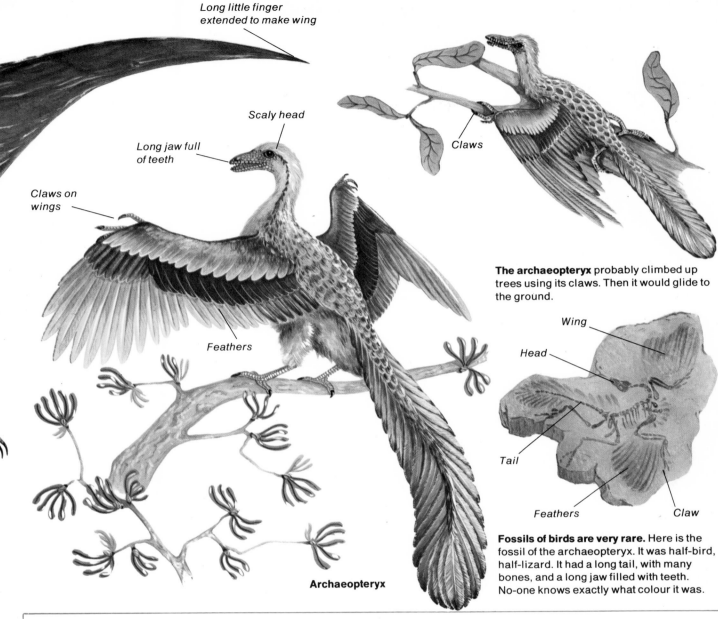

Long little finger extended to make wing

Scaly head

Long jaw full of teeth

Claws on wings

Feathers

Claws

Archaeopteryx

The archaeopteryx probably climbed up trees using its claws. Then it would glide to the ground.

Wing

Head

Tail

Feathers

Claw

Fossils of birds are very rare. Here is the fossil of the archaeopteryx. It was half-bird, half-lizard. It had a long tail, with many bones, and a long jaw filled with teeth. No-one knows exactly what colour it was.

Evolution

The slow change which happens to living things over a long time has a special name. It is called evolution. Evolution happens because animals and plants must change to be able to survive.

Change for the Better

When birds started to fly, they could escape more easily from their enemies. They could build their nests in trees and keep their offspring safe. The birds which survived were those which adapted best to their surroundings. The birds they produced were also well-adapted. The other weaker birds died out. This process is called natural selection.

Charles Darwin

In the last century, a British scientist called Charles Darwin visited the Galapagos Islands, off the coast of South America. He saw finches on all the islands, but they were all different. He worked out that the first finches to arrive on the islands had all looked alike. Then they had adapted in different ways to life on the various Galapagos Islands. Charles Darwin was the first person to work out how and why evolution happened.

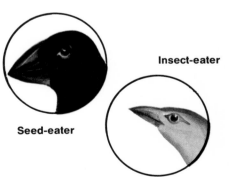

Insect-eater

Seed-eater

The finches of the Galapagos Islands all vary greatly. Notice how their beaks have changed according to the food they eat. Seed-eating finches have short, stout beaks to crack seeds open. Insect-eating finches have sharp, pointed beaks to pick out insects and beetles from tree-bark.

How Birds Die Out

Many sorts of birds no longer exist. They have either been wiped out by natural causes, or by man.

Hunters sometimes kill too many birds. The birds may die out as a result.

Cities are built on land which once provided food and shelter for many birds.

The dodo was a kind of pigeon. It lived on the island of Mauritius, in the Indian Ocean. It was killed by the dogs and pigs which sailors took to the island. It could not fly to escape. Men killed the dodo, too, for food.

The dodo became extinct about 300 years ago. Just before, one was brought to London and put on show. The keeper fed it pebbles, and it died of starvation.

Extinction

Since life began, thousands of different kinds of animals have died out. When an animal dies out, it becomes extinct. Experts do not know all the reasons why animals become extinct. Sometimes, however, it is man's fault.

Hunted to Death

Since man appeared on earth, he has killed off many animals by hunting them for food, or for their fur, or because they were fierce and dangerous.

If men hunt animals in great numbers, the animals sometimes die out completely: The passenger pigeon, once very numerous, was killed off during the nineteenth century, because men hunted it for food.

Other animals died out when man began to till the land. This destroyed the places where animals live.

When men build cities, they take away the trees and woodland where birds and other animals live and breed. The area in which animals can safely live and breed becomes smaller and smaller.

Pollution

Today, there is another danger. Chemicals are used to protect crops from diseases. Some of these chemicals are dangerous to animals. Waste products, like oil, are also being dumped into rivers and in the seas. The water is being poisoned, or polluted. Many birds and other animals all over the world are dying because of the effects of pollution.

More animals are becoming extinct today than ever before.

Protection

In some countries, there are national parks, where animals can live and breed in safety. There are also many bird sanctuaries, where the birds are protected by law. Many sorts of birds, however, are still on the brink of extinction.

The great auk lived in the North Atlantic. Like the penguin, it could swim, but it could not fly. The last great auk died on June 4, 1844. It was largely killed off by man.

The passenger pigeon of North America was so numerous that the flocks darkened the sky. Men killed it for food. The last one died on September 1, 1914.

The Labrador duck lived on the Atlantic coast of North America. The last one was killed on Long Island, New York, in 1875.

Moas were large, flightless birds living in New Zealand. Some were taller than a man. The Maoris hunted them. Towards the end of the 18th century the moas were extinct.

The huia, another New Zealand bird, has not been seen since 1907. Changes in the forest caused its extinction. It was also hunted too much.

The elephant bird lived in Madagascar, and became extinct several thousand years ago. The bird was much taller than a man. It weighed nearly half a ton (0.5 tonnes).

The Carolina parakeet was killed in large numbers for its beautiful feathers. It was also good to eat, and therefore often killed for food.

The ivory-billed woodpecker of North America became very scarce because many forests were cut down. It was thought to be extinct, but a few pairs were found in 1966.

The solitaire, first cousin to the dodo, lived on the island of Réunion, in the Indian Ocean. Only its skeleton remains to show what it looked like.

How Birds Fly

**In true flight, a bird beats its wings to stay in the air.
Some birds glide, using air currents more than wing beats.**

The first thing a bird does when it is about to take off is to lower its body, bend its legs and spread its wings. Then it straightens its legs and takes a jump into the air. It starts to beat its wings immediately.

Once airborne, the bird must push its wings downwards to give itself lift. The large feathers of the wing, called the primaries, are held together so that there are no gaps between them to let the air through.

The Feather

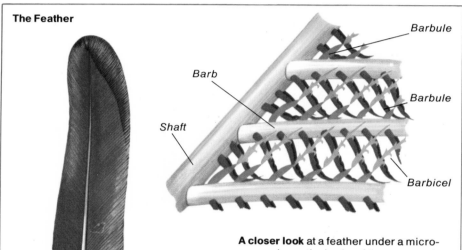

Barbule

Barb

Barbule

Shaft

Barbicel

Vane, made up of barbs

Shaft, or quill

A closer look at a feather under a microscope shows the barbs of the vane, and the little overlapping barbules on each barb. The barbules carry smaller barbicels, which have hooked ends. The tiny hooks of the barbicels make the barbules interlock. This forms the very delicate, but very strong, smooth vane. When a feather looks ruffled, the barbs have become unhooked.

A feather is made up of a shaft and a vane. The shaft is the central stem of the feather. The vane is made up of rows of barbs set close together on either side of the shaft. The barbs are hooked together to give a smooth surface to the feather.

The soft feathers which cover a chick are called down. Down feathers do not interlock. Adult birds have an undercoat of down to keep them warm when they fly.

Development of Flight

The very first birds could not fly well. Their wings were not very strong, and their bones were not the right shape.

In time, most birds grew longer arms and more feathers to help them to fly better. The bones became hollow and weighed less. Birds developed pockets inside their bodies to hold more air and make them light. These pockets are called air-sacs.

Airborne

The wing feathers open and close as a bird moves its wings to fly. On a downbeat, the feathers are tightly closed to push against the air underneath. On the upbeat, they re-open to let the air through. In this way, the bird does not have to work hard to push against the air above to raise its wings.

Gliding

True flight is powered. This means the wings beat up and down to keep the bird in the air. Some birds, however, do not beat their wings all the time when they are in the air. They use breezes and currents of air to move them along and keep them aloft. This sort of flying is called gliding. Gliding birds usually have very long wings to allow them to catch as much of the air current or breeze as possible.

At the end of the downstroke, the wings are lifted for the upstroke. They become flexible and curved instead of rigid, as in the downstroke. This makes it easier for the muscles to lift the wings. The primaries open slightly, leaving gaps through which the air can pass.

After completing the upstroke, the wings become rigid again. The primaries are closed to stop air coming through. The wings present a solid surface to the air underneath. The large flight muscles now pull the wing down again in a repeat of the downbeat.

Gliding and Hovering

The albatross can glide for thousands of miles without a wing beat. It has very long wings, and lives over the oceans. It uses the upcurrents of air from the waves to lift itself up and stay aloft.

Vultures make use of columns of warm air to glide in the sky. These columns of air are called thermals. They rise from the ground as it is heated by the sun. The vultures stay up with the thermals until they see a dead or dying animal which they can eat. Then they drop down on their prey.

The kestrel, or windhover, feeds mainly on mice, insects and earthworms. It stays motionless in the sky with its head into the wind, watching for something to eat.

Hummingbirds hover in front of flowers to suck up the nectar. When a bird hovers, its wings move rapidly backwards and forwards, and it stays in one place. Hummingbird wings beat up to 80 times a second.

The Senses of a Bird

Birds spend most of their lives looking for food and watching out for enemies. Sight is therefore their most important sense.

Seeing

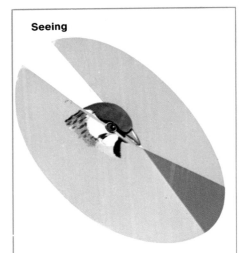

Birds that eat seeds, berries and insects must be able to see in colour to find their food easily. They must also be able to see over a wide area. Their eyes are on the sides of the head, so that they can search either side for food. They are also able to keep watch all round for enemies. They cannot see much in front of their beaks, so they sometimes fly into windows or poles.

Birds that feed by night are hunters of small, quick-moving animals. They have to see small movements to catch their prey. The best eye for this is one which sees only shades of grey, like a non-colour television screen. These birds hunt at night, in the dark, so they do not need colour vision. They need eyes in the front of their heads to be able to judge how far an animal is away.

Owls hunt by night. To help them, they have large eyes which can see well even in dim light. The eyes take up most of the room in an owl's head.

The Senses

A bird's most important sense is sight. Most birds have a very poor sense of smell.

Keen Vision

The eyes of some birds, like hawks, are about ten times as keen as human eyes. Hawks are hunters, and their eyes are in the front of their heads. In this way they can easily watch their prey moving without having to turn their heads.

Side Vision

Smaller birds that feed on seeds, berries and insects, have eyes at the sides of the head. They can see what is happening to their left and to their right. They can look on both sides for food, and keep watch for enemies.

Day birds see in colour, but night birds see only in shades of grey.

Hearing

Birds have no ear flaps like humans to direct sound waves into the ear. Their ear openings are actually covered with feathers. Yet they can hear very well. Many of them, however, cannot pick up the direction of sound very easily.

Owls can pick up direction well, because their inside ear is made in a special way. They can listen out for their prey.

A parrot is a day bird. Its eyes are set on either side of its head to watch for food and enemies. It has to turn its head sideways to look straight ahead with one eye.

Hearing

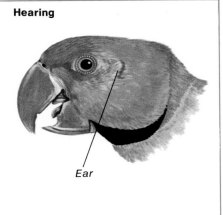

Ear

The opening to a parrot's ear, like most birds, is covered with feathers. Nevertheless, a parrot can hear very well. It is a good mimic, and can imitate even quite small sounds.

An owl hunting for food at night uses sight and hearing to catch its prey. Some owls can catch mice in total darkness, just by listening for movement.

Smelling

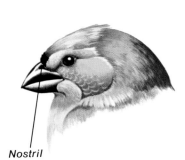

Nostril

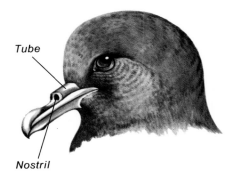

Tube

Nostril

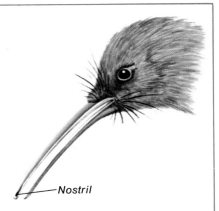

Nostril

The nostrils of most birds are on the top of the beak. They are used mainly for breathing, and not for smelling. A bird's sense of smell is usually poor.

Petrels are seabirds. They have a good sense of smell. Petrels eat fish, and can smell dead fish floating some way away. The tube on the nose picks up the smell.

The kiwi finds earthworms at night by pushing its long beak into the ground. Its nostrils are at the end of the beak. It can smell the worms underground.

Can Birds Think?

Birds live mainly by instinct. They do not often have to work things out, but they can solve simple problems if necessary.

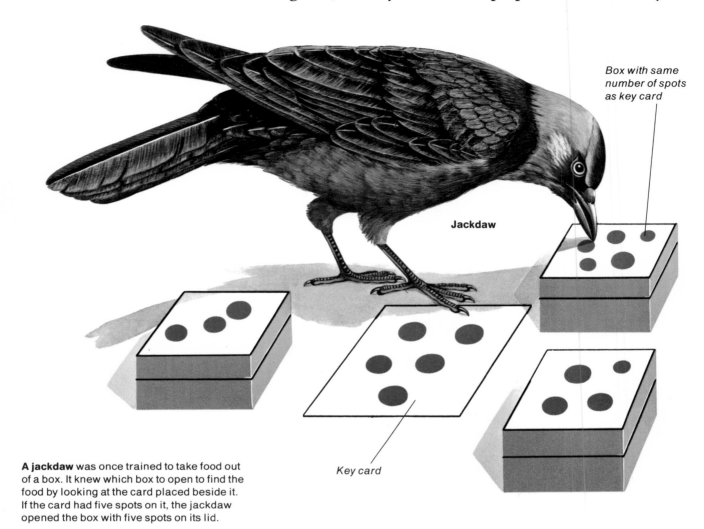

Box with same number of spots as key card

Jackdaw

Key card

A jackdaw was once trained to take food out of a box. It knew which box to open to find the food by looking at the card placed beside it. If the card had five spots on it, the jackdaw opened the box with five spots on its lid.

Instinct

Nearly everything an animal does is instinctive. An animal does not have to learn to do things, nor copy other animals. Something inside itself tells it what to do. This is called insight, but people prefer to call it intelligence.

If an egg is hatched in an incubator, it means the chick is reared on its own in a special warm box. It does not have a mother to show it what to do. Yet it will feed itself. Later it will make a nest. It can do all this without ever seeing another bird. It is all instinctive.

Learning

Sometimes, a bird learns what to do from its mistakes. This is called learning by trial and error. As soon as a farmyard chick is hatched, it pecks at anything. Some things are good to eat, some are not. The chick tries each one out. Soon, it learns what is good to eat and what is bad just by looking.

Problems

Besides using instinct, and learning by trial and error, birds can solve simple problems. To show this, scientists have made little boxes, which can only be opened by pulling a string or handle. They put a peanut in the box, and put the box on a bird table. Along comes a small bird. It looks at the box for a moment, then pulls the string or the handle. The bird has worked out how to get the food. It has solved the problem. This is called using intelligence.

Clever Tricks

Birds spend most of their lives trying to find food. Their instinct is usually enough for this. They do not often need to use intelligence. Yet when a bird is tame and living with people, it often learns to do things it would never do in the wild. This is partly because it no longer has to hunt for its food. So it can give more attention to other things.

Problem Solving

A gull cannot crack open a hard mussel with its beak. It flies up into the air with the mussel and drops it from a height on to the rocks to break it.

The woodpecker finch of the Galapagos Islands uses a tool. It breaks off a cactus spine, holds it in its beak, and uses it to pick out insects hiding in tree-bark.

Blue tits can draw up peanuts hung on a string. They lift the string with their beak and place it under one foot. They repeat this until the nuts are on the perch, and they can eat them.

Many birds can copy words. Parrots, budgerigars and mynahs are good talkers. They can often link a word with an action, but they do not understand the word. A pet parrot in a house will say 'hello' when the telephone bell rings. It will also copy the voice of the person answering the call.

Birds can copy other sounds, too. Once, some woodmen were felling trees with a power saw. They stopped for lunch, but the sound of the saw continued. A starling in a tree nearby was copying the saw. Then the starling made an astonishing mixture of noises. They were the sounds of a tree falling. There was the rustle of leaves, the crack of breaking branches, and the final thud as the trunk hit the ground. The starling could repeat all these sounds over and over again.

Budgerigar

Mynah

How a Nest is Built

Birds build nests as a protected place in which to lay their eggs and bring up their young.

Plover pivots to make nest

The male ringed plover courts the female by crouching in front of her. He turns round and round, scratching at the sand with his feet.

The nest is just a scrape in the sand

As the plover turns, he makes a shallow scrape in the sandy earth. The female lines this nest with stones, shells, or dried plants.

Lining of shells *Eggs are hard to see*

The four eggs are the colour of stone, with dark brown and grey marks. They look like pebbles and are very hard to find.

Goldfinch collects materials for the nest

The hen goldfinch builds the nest on her own. The male stands and watches. The nest is in a tree or hedge.

Lining of down and wool

The goldfinch nest is made of roots, grass, moss and lichen. It is lined with down and wool, and sometimes with hair.

Cup-shaped nest stops eggs falling out

Five or six eggs are laid by the hen. They are bluish-white with spots and streaks of red-brown.

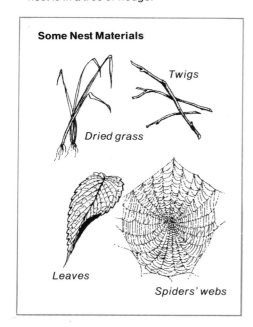

Some Nest Materials

Twigs

Dried grass

Leaves

Spiders' webs

Two Ways to Nest

Some birds always build their nests on the ground, others always build them in trees or bushes. Nests on the ground are less safe than nests in trees. All eggs laid by birds that nest on the ground have special colours and patterns to make them hard to see.

Building the Nest

Both parent birds usually build the nest. Sometimes the female builds it by herself. Some birds take only a few hours to build a nest, others take days because the nest is more difficult to make.

Birds usually build new nests every year. Some birds, like swal-lows, come back to the same nest each year

Nest Materials

Most nests are made of several things. Dried grass and sticks are the most common. Mud is often used, too. Usually, there are four or five kinds of material, with a softer kind for the lining, like moss and feathers.

Some of the very small song birds use spiders' webs, either to bind other materials together, or sometimes to make the whole nest.

Sea birds often use seaweeds for their nests. Most penguins use pebbles. The cave swifts of Asia make their nests of their own saliva.

The Baya weaver lives in south-east Asia. The cock weaves a nest of grass in a tree. It looks like a bottle hanging upside down. The hen lines the nest with down and feathers.

The emperor penguin lives in Antarctica. It does not make a nest. The parents take turns holding the egg on their feet to keep it off the cold ground.

The tailor bird lives in south-east Asia. The male sews two large leaves together with plant fibres or spiders' webs. Each stitch is tied in a knot.

The female hornbill nests in a hollow tree. The opening to the nest is walled up with mud, leaving only a tiny slit. The male brings her the mud. He swallows it first, then coughs it up to give to her. She breaks out of the nest when her chicks are ready to fly.

Winning a Mate

Birds must find a mate when the breeding season starts. The male birds court the females by singing, dancing and showing off.

The drake, or male mallard, performs a dance when he courts his mate, lifting his wings and tail.

The drake also bobs his head up and down, bowing to the female, who is called the duck.

The duck replies by stretching her neck out of the water as though she were drinking.

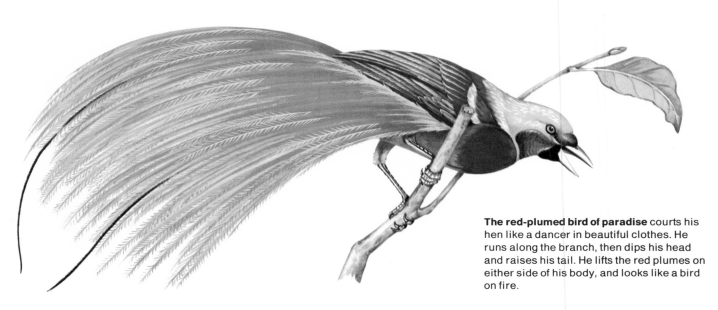

The red-plumed bird of paradise courts his hen like a dancer in beautiful clothes. He runs along the branch, then dips his head and raises his tail. He lifts the red plumes on either side of his body, and looks like a bird on fire.

Showing Off

Male birds start looking for a mate at the beginning of the breeding season. The males are often very much more beautiful than the females. Their plumage, which means all the feathers on their body, often has brilliant patches of colour. Sometimes their tails are much longer than those of the females. Some male birds have tufts of feathers, or ruffs, which make them more beautiful. They show off this beautiful plumage to the females.

Courtship

Showing off brilliant patches of colour to the females is the beginning of a courtship. Male birds with long feathers, like peacocks, raise them in a fan. Often, they dance or strut in front of the female.

Singing

Birds also sing to attract a mate. Crows, which usually make harsh, cawing noises, use soft, sweet sounds when courting.

Gifts

Besides singing to his mate, the male bird sometimes brings her gifts. He may bring her food in his beak, and she opens her beak to receive it. Sometimes he may pick up a piece of stick and offer it to her. It looks like a suggestion to start making a nest.

Making Friends

During their courtship, the birds get to know each other better. They can tell whether they like each other enough to live together.

Setting Up House

Bird courtship is more than just making friends. It is also the time when the partners choose where to build a nest and bring up their young. Sometimes the hen builds the nest by herself, and sometimes the cock does all the building. Most birds work as partners. One bird collects the material, and the other builds the nest.

The peacock, or male peafowl, has long feathers in front of his tail. These are called his train. To attract the peahen he raises it in a magnificent fan. He struts in front of the peahen, showing off his beauty. Sometimes he rattles his train.

The crestless gardener makes a special place in which to court the female. It is a hut or bower made of sticks piled up around a small tree. He lays out a garden in front of it, with flowers. He even makes a hedge of sticks.

The Birth of a Bird

During the breeding season, birds mate in pairs, build their nests, and lay their eggs. Most birds do this once a year.

Male and female birds must mate before the hen can lay an egg. When they mate, the male bird mounts the female. He brings the opening at the end of his body down to touch her opening. Then he sends a fluid into her body. This fluid contains millions of sperms, so tiny that they can only be seen under a microscope.

Inside the hen is the ovary. The ovary contains the beginning of an egg, called the egg-cell. The egg-cell fills up with yolk and leaves the ovary. It passes into a tube, where it meets a sperm. The sperm enters the egg-cell, and this is how a chick begins. The egg collects white and shell from the glands it passes on its way to be laid.

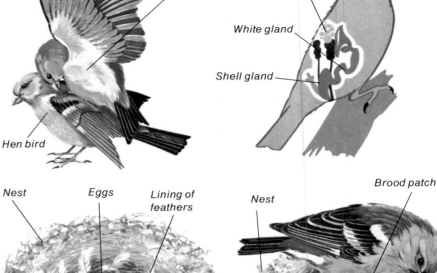

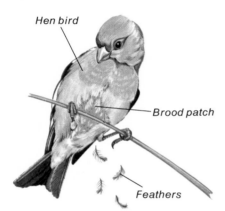

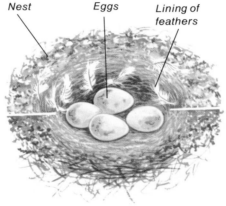

Before the egg is laid, a patch on the hen's breast begins to itch. The feathers drop out, or are pulled out by the hen. This bare spot is called the brood patch. It has many blood vessels which make it warm.

Many birds line their nest with feathers. The feathers make the nest cosy and warm for the hen and the chicks. They make a soft and very warm lining for the eggs when they are laid.

Once all the eggs are laid, the hen begins to sit, or crouch, on them. As she does this, her warm brood patch touches the eggs. The eggs are kept warm by the feathers below, and the heat from the brood patch above.

Inside an egg, you can see the white and the yolk. The white protects the yolk. The yolk is food for the developing chick, which is just a little spot in the yolk to begin with. Fresh air can pass through the egg shell so that the growing chick can breathe. Thick ropes of white hold the egg yolk. Because these ropes are twisted, the yolk can turn round. This means that the growing chick always faces upwards, towards the heat of the hen's body.

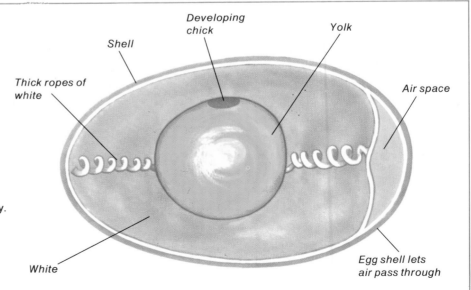

The Breeding Season

Birds mate at a special time of the year. This is called their breeding season. This is the time when food needed for their babies is easily found.

A male and female form a pair. They mate, and after this the female lays her eggs. The chicks develop in the eggs laid in the nest. They do not develop inside her. If the hen carried her growing babies inside her, she would be too heavy to fly.

Egg Cells

Each baby starts as a single cell, called the egg-cell. The egg-cell will grow into a chick only if another cell, known as the sperm-cell, from the male, joins with it. It then divides again and again into hundreds of cells. These make up the body of the chick. Some cells form the muscles, some form the bones, others form the brain, heart and lungs, and so on.

Laying the Eggs

The time between mating and egg-laying is different for different birds. It may take one day, or several days. The time taken for the egg to be laid is different, too. The cuckoo takes only a few seconds to lay an egg. Other birds take one minute, three minutes, or ten minutes. A turkey or goose can take two hours.

When Are Eggs Laid?

Some birds lay eggs at special times. Finches, wrens and hummingbirds lay at sunrise. Pigeons lay in the afternoon. Pheasants lay in the evening. Only one egg is laid at a time. The next egg is laid the next day, or sometimes two or three days later. Some birds lay one egg a week. Some hens will go on laying if the eggs are taken away. A sparrow usually lays four or five eggs, but it can lay as many as fifty if the eggs are taken away as soon as they are laid.

The farmyard hen does the same thing. Its ancestors were wild jungle fowl, and because they laid so many eggs, people kept them as farmyard animals.

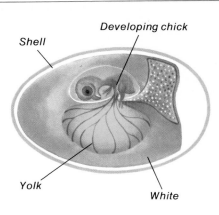

Shell *Developing chick* *Yolk* *White*

Eggs must always be kept warm so that the chicks can grow inside. They must be at a temperature of 34 degrees centigrade, which is nearly as warm as the human body.

The growing chick uses up the yolk as food. At the same time the white begins to dry up. If the egg stays cold for more than an hour or two, the chick dies.

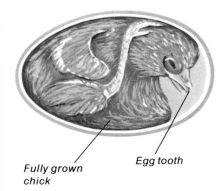

Fully grown chick *Egg tooth*

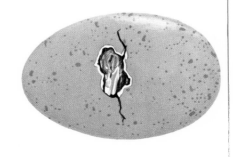

The chick grows until it fills the shell. It is then ready to hatch out. It has a tiny tooth on the end of its beak, called an egg tooth.

The chick taps on the shell with its egg tooth when it is ready to hatch. The shell begins to crack, and the chick starts to push with its head.

A cap of shell drops off, and the chick can take deep breaths. The chick is tired, so it rests for a bit inside the shell, before struggling free. Its egg tooth drops off.

The chick is wet at first from what is left of the white. Its fluffy down soon dries out, and the chick begins to feed. It pecks at anything looking like a seed.

Why are Eggs Different?

All birds lay eggs. The eggs are all different in shape, size and colour, and fit in with their surroundings.

Owl's Egg

Owl

Plover's Egg

Plover

Guillemot's Egg

Guillemot

An owl nests in dark places, like hollow trees. The eggs are white. No colour is needed to hide them, as they are already well hidden. The eggs (below) are round, but cannot roll far as there is not much space in the nest.

A plover's nest looks like a shallow saucer in sandy ground. Plovers' eggs are coloured to match their surroundings (see below). Otherwise, enemies could see them easily. This colouring is called camouflage.

Guillemots' eggs are laid on a bare cliff ledge. They are pear-shaped, so if moved, they just roll in a circle. They cannot fall off the ledge of the cliff (see below). The eggs are camouflaged to hide them from enemies.

Owl's Nest

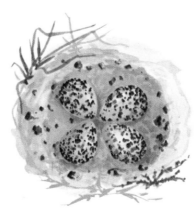

Plover's Nest

Guillemot's Nest

Why Eggs?

Birds do not carry their babies inside them because they would be too heavy to fly far. Some animals that fly, like bats, carry their babies until they are born alive. But bats do not fly as much or as far as birds.

Kinds of Eggs

There are over 8,000 different kinds of birds, and there are as many different kinds of eggs. The eggs are all different shapes, sizes and colours.

Usually, the smaller the bird, the smaller the egg. Birds which lay large eggs for their size lay fewer eggs. A kiwi, for example, lays an egg that is one-eighth of its own size, but it usually lays only one.

The little hummingbird, only two inches or so long, lays several eggs, but they are all small in proportion to its size.

Shapes of Eggs

Most birds' eggs have a blunt end and a more pointed end. This shape is called "oviform". It is the best shape for packing eggs into a small space. This egg shape does not roll along like a ball. It rolls in small circles because it is not round. So if an egg rolls out of a nest on the ground, it will not go far, and the hen can get it back. Only eggs laid in hollows are nearly round. Eggs laid in nests above the ground are rounder than those laid on the ground.

Colours of Eggs

The colours of birds' eggs show the kinds of nests in which they were laid. Some nests are in holes in trees or in a bank, and very little light reaches them. Eggs laid in these dark nests are white. There is no need for colour in darkness.

Other eggs have white or coloured shells decorated with coloured spots or lines. They break up the outline of the egg so that it is hard for enemies to see. This is called camouflage. These eggs are laid in the open, in nests on the ground, in trees, or on rock ledges, and so it is important that they are well hidden.

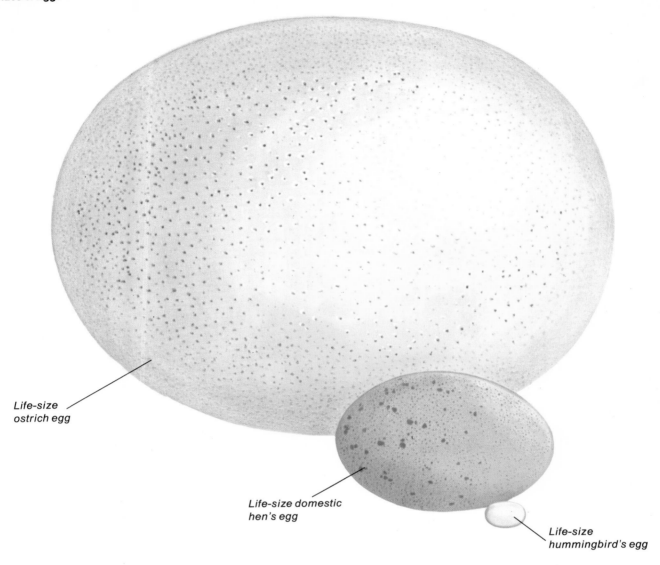

Life-size ostrich egg

Life-size domestic hen's egg

Life-size hummingbird's egg

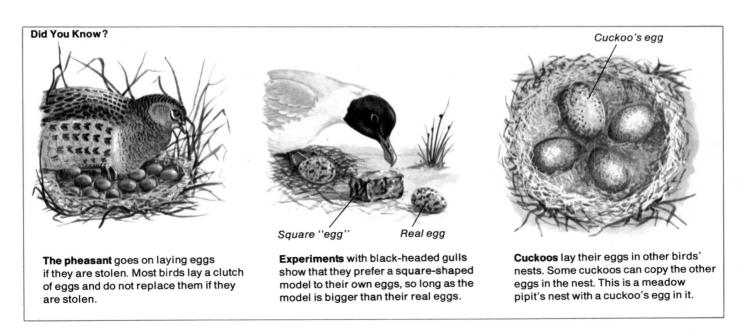

Did You Know?

Square "egg" *Real egg*

Cuckoo's egg

The pheasant goes on laying eggs if they are stolen. Most birds lay a clutch of eggs and do not replace them if they are stolen.

Experiments with black-headed gulls show that they prefer a square-shaped model to their own eggs, so long as the model is bigger than their real eggs.

Cuckoos lay their eggs in other birds' nests. Some cuckoos can copy the other eggs in the nest. This is a meadow pipit's nest with a cuckoo's egg in it.

Growing Up

Birds born on the ground can look after themselves soon after birth. Birds born off the ground need much more parental care.

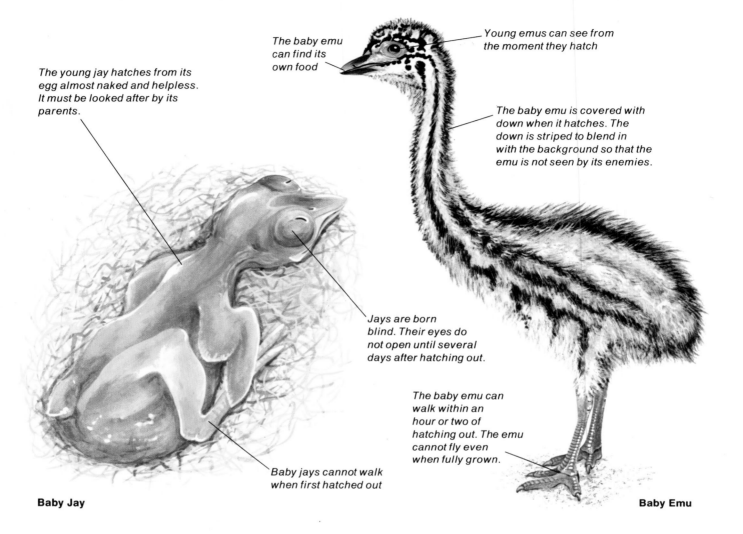

The young jay hatches from its egg almost naked and helpless. It must be looked after by its parents.

The baby emu can find its own food

Young emus can see from the moment they hatch

The baby emu is covered with down when it hatches. The down is striped to blend in with the background so that the emu is not seen by its enemies.

Jays are born blind. Their eyes do not open until several days after hatching out.

The baby emu can walk within an hour or two of hatching out. The emu cannot fly even when fully grown.

Baby jays cannot walk when first hatched out

Baby Jay

Baby Emu

Nest in tree

Cat on the prowl

Nest on ground

A nest in a tree is never quite safe. It is a little safer than a nest on the ground. A cat on the prowl can easily find a nest on the ground. It would have to look hard for one in a tree, and also climb up the tree to find it.

Born on the Ground

Young birds that are hatched in a nest on the ground are usually able to run about when they are only an hour old. They can also feed themselves. Their bodies are covered with downy feathers. Their parents still keep a watchful eye on them, but the young birds can do a lot for themselves.

Born off the Ground

Birds hatched in nests in trees or bushes are naked and blind at first. They are fed for two weeks or more by their parents. The parents push food, usually caterpillars or other insects, down the young birds' throats.

Camouflage

Birds hatched on the ground are in greater danger than those hatched in nests in trees or bushes. They need protection from enemies on the ground as well as in the air. They also risk being trodden on. Two things protect these young birds. Their down is usually camouflaged to blend in with their background, and make them hard to see. Also, they freeze perfectly still at the first sign of danger, instead of flying away. When they freeze they are even more difficult to find.

Young birds are protected from some enemies by instinct. Their parents also teach them that some animals are dangerous.

Baby birds born in trees are naked and blind when they hatch. They are fed by their parents. They open their beaks whenever the nest is shaken. They know the parent has landed on a twig nearby with food in its beak.

Baby birds born on the ground run about as soon as they are hatched. They pick up food right away. They peck by instinct at anything but have to learn what is good to eat and what is not. The hen often shows them the good food.

Baby birds born naked leave the nest when they have grown their first feathers. They are then called fledglings. They sit on the edge of the nest or on a branch and beat their wings. This is the first step in learning to fly.

When a baby magpie hatches, it has no feathers and is blind and helpless.

The young magpie leaves the nest covered with feathers. Its tail is very short, because it is still young.

Here is a fully grown magpie with all its feathers. Magpies look black and white, but close up the black is a beautiful blue-green.

27

How Birds Eat

Different birds eat different things. There are five main sources of food, and a great variety of beaks to cope with them.

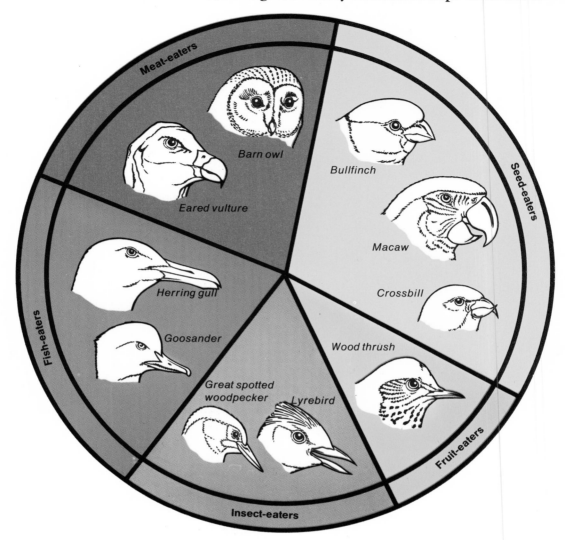

Meat-eaters

Barn owl

Eared vulture

Seed-eaters

Bullfinch

Macaw

Crossbill

Herring gull

Goosander

Fish-eaters

Wood thrush

Great spotted woodpecker

Lyrebird

Fruit-eaters

Insect-eaters

Beaks

Birds do not have any teeth to bite and chew their food. Therefore their beaks are very important. The shape of a bird's beak shows the sort of food the bird eats.

Seed-Eaters

Seed-eating birds, like the finches, have short beaks ending in a point. The beak is strong enough to crack the husks or shells of seeds.

Macaws belong to the parrot family. They eat nuts, which are a kind of seed. Macaws can crack brazil nuts.

The crossbill picks seeds out of pine cones. The crossed bill is used to prise open the cones.

Fruit-Eaters

Many kinds of birds eat fruit such as berries, or soft fruit like plums, pears and apples. Some birds, like parrots, eat mainly nuts but sometimes feed on fruit. True fruit-eaters are birds like thrushes. They have a fairly long bill but it is not very strong. Fruit-eaters like thrushes are called soft-billed birds.

Insect-Eaters

Soft-billed birds and seed-eaters will eat insects from time to time. Some birds, however, eat mainly insects.

Swallows catch insects on the wing. They have very short bills and they can open their mouths wide to catch the insects.

Birds which pick insects up from the ground have long, fairly thin beaks, like the lyrebird of Australia.

Woodpeckers eat insect grubs out of wood. They hack a hole in the wood to reach the grub. Their beaks are long and strong, like a pick.

Fish-Eaters

Fishes can move quickly and they have slimy bodies. Birds like the ducks called goosanders and mergansers have horny teeth along the edges of their bills, for holding slippery fish.

Not all fish-eating birds have these special beaks. Gulls catch fish and their beaks are slightly hooked

A kiwi's bill is long and flexible. It can be used to search for food. The nostrils are right at the end of the bill. The kiwi pushes its bill into the ground and searches for earthworms. It finds the worms partly by touch, but mainly by smelling them out with its nostrils.

Other birds also have very special beaks. The hummingbird has a long, slender bill to push down into large flowers to suck the nectar.

A pelican has a large bag of skin under its beak. The pelican feeds on fish, and the bag acts like a fishing net.

In Africa, there is a bird called the oxpecker. It depends on other animals for its food in a rather special way. It runs over the backs of antelopes, zebras and buffalos, picking off the ticks which suck blood from the large animal's skin. In this way it helps both the large animal, by removing the ticks, and also it helps itself by finding food.

Relying on other animals to provide food is called interdependence. There is interdependence throughout the animal kingdom. Animals either eat other animals, or plants. If this balance is upset, whole species may be threatened with extinction. If, for example, too many dangerous chemicals are used on the land, they may kill off plants and animals. Other animals which normally feed on these plants and animals can no longer find food. So they are threatened with extinction.

at the end to hold the fish. Kingfishers and herons have long, strong beaks, shaped like a dagger. This kind of beak acts like a large pair of tweezers.

Meat-Eaters

There are two kinds of meat-eating birds. The first kind, like owls, hawks, eagles and falcons, catch their prey alive. They have hooked beaks which are short and strong. The second kind are vultures, which eat the flesh of dead animals. Their beaks are also hooked but are not so short as the first kind. Both birds use their beaks for tearing up flesh. They hold the flesh under their feet, called talons, and tear it with their beaks.

Gulls eat mussels they find on the shore when the tide is out. A mussel has a hard shell. The gulls fly up and drop the mussels onto rocks to break the shell.

Vultures cannot break the hard shell of an ostrich egg with their beaks. To eat the egg, the Egyptian vulture drops a stone onto the egg to break the shell.

Inside a Bird

A bird's body, outside and inside, is specially adapted for life on the wing.

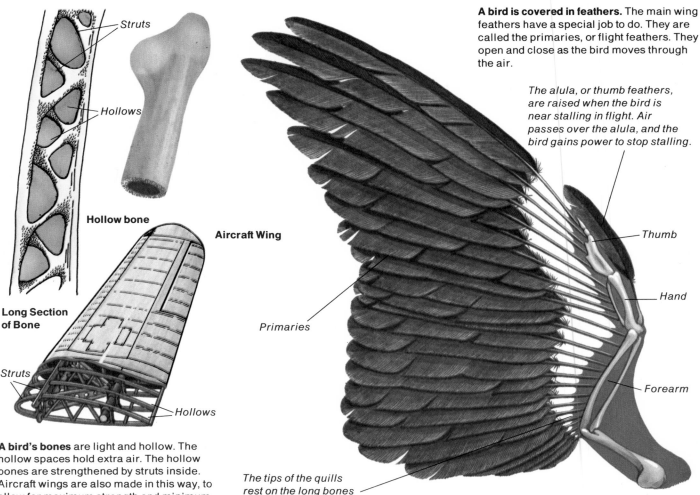

Struts

Hollows

Hollows

Hollow bone

Long Section of Bone

Aircraft Wing

Struts

Hollows

A bird's bones are light and hollow. The hollow spaces hold extra air. The hollow bones are strengthened by struts inside. Aircraft wings are also made in this way, to allow for maximum strength and minimum weight.

A bird is covered in feathers. The main wing feathers have a special job to do. They are called the primaries, or flight feathers. They open and close as the bird moves through the air.

The alula, or thumb feathers, are raised when the bird is near stalling in flight. Air passes over the alula, and the bird gains power to stop stalling.

Thumb

Hand

Forearm

Primaries

The tips of the quills rest on the long bones of the forearm and hand.

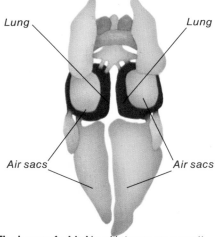

Lung

Lung

Air sacs

Air sacs

The lungs of a bird lead into a very complicated system of bags of air, called air sacs. These sacs hold extra air, to keep the bird light and allow it to take in plenty of oxygen.

Flying

Most birds can fly. Their bodies are very light and completely adapted in all sorts of ways to help them fly easily. Their bones are light and hollow. They have strong muscles to move their wings.

Keeping Warm

It can be very cold flying at high speed. Some birds fly at speeds of 100 m.p.h. (161 k.p.h.) and so they have small feathers underneath their outside layer of feathers. These are called down feathers. They form a sort of inner jacket which keeps the bird warm. The working muscles also produce heat to keep the bird warm.

Keeping Cool

The large flight muscles of a bird use up a lot of energy. So although a bird may be cold when flying high, it may also get very hot in normal flight, because of all the hard work it has to do. It cannot shed its coat to keep cool. It cannot perspire because it has no sweat glands like humans. It has an inside cooling system, using the lungs and air sacs. As the air is breathed in, it passes into the lungs and then into the air sacs, which lie between the organs of the body and in the bones. The used air, when breathed out, carries away heat and keeps the bird cool.

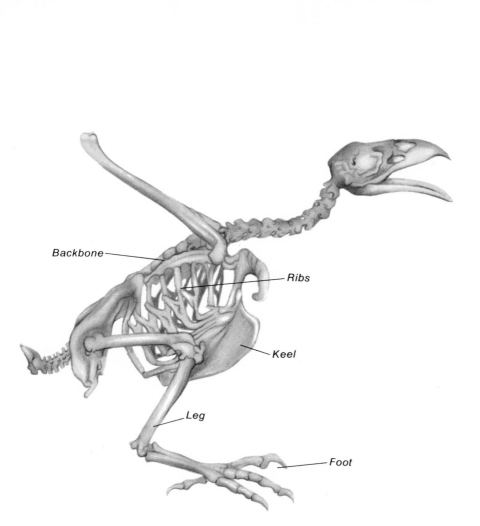

Backbone

Ribs

Keel

Leg

Foot

The large breast muscle on each side of the keel on the breastbone is very strong. It moves the wing in flight.

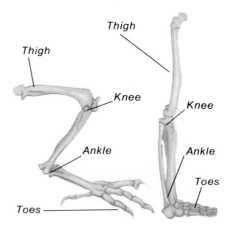

Thigh

Thigh

Knee

Knee

Ankle

Ankle

Toes

Toes

The skeleton of a bird is like a cage holding the body firm for flying. It has long wing bones. The long legs are like an under-carriage, to be let down when the bird lands.

A bird's knee is hidden under its body feathers. What looks like its knee is really its ankle. Compare it with the skeleton of a man's leg.

A bird digests food in a special way. When a bird eats, it does not always have time to digest its food, because it has to fly off quickly to escape from its enemies. So a bird has a storage place inside its body, called the crop. Food goes first to the crop, and stays there until ready to be digested. Then the food moves to the gizzard, or stomach of the bird. People have teeth to chew food up before it goes into the stomach, but birds do not. Instead, the muscles of the gizzard move the food around and grind it up small. Seed-eating birds sometimes swallow grit to help the gizzard to grind up the food. A bird gets rid of waste matter through the back passage, or cloaca. Some birds do not have a gizzard. Birds that eat flesh do not need a gizzard because flesh is easy to digest.

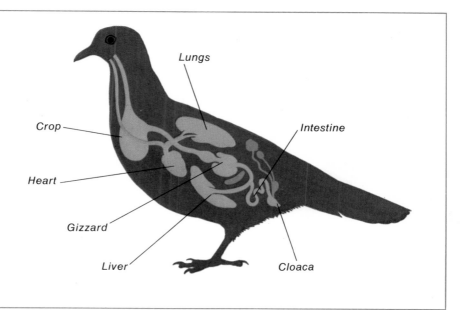

Lungs

Crop

Intestine

Heart

Gizzard

Liver

Cloaca

Private Property

At the beginning of the breeding season, birds find a piece of land which becomes their own private property.

Sea birds have very small territories. Each territory is only a small space round each nest. There is plenty of food in the sea, so no more land is needed.

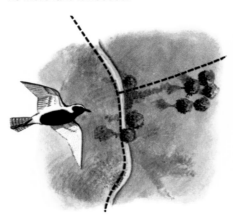

A plover flies over a field, showing the boundaries of other plovers' territories. These are sometimes more crowded than here.

Birds like swallows catch insects on the wing, and so they need no territory. There is plenty of food for them in the air.

A golden eagle's territory is often three miles (4.8 km.) across. It is difficult for birds of prey to find food. They do not catch every small animal they chase. Also, if they hunted over a small area, they would clean it out.

Flocks

During winter, small birds stay together in flocks. In spring the flocks begin to break up as the males leave the flock for a short while each day. Each male finds a place on a branch in a tree or bush. As the days pass, he spends more and more time on the same branch. He begins to sing in several places around the tree. These places are called song posts. They mark the boundary of the piece of land which the bird calls his own. It is called his territory. The male sings to warn other birds that the land is his private property. He fights any male of his own kind that tries to come into his territory.

Setting Up House

Soon, a female hears him sing, and likes his voice. She goes into his territory. At first, he fights her as if she was another male. She does not fight back, and he lets her stay. If she likes his territory she stays and becomes his mate.

Feeding

The territory becomes the feeding ground for the two birds. They keep other birds out, to be sure they will not take their food. The territory must be large enough to provide food for the babies also, when they hatch out.

Fighting Birds

Birds usually only fight over property. Often, a simple warning is enough to frighten other birds away.

Small birds, like wagtails, spring into the air trying to scratch with their claws as they fight. Most fighting is between male birds.

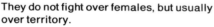

They do not fight over females, but usually over territory.

Birds of prey, like the falcon, have large claws called talons. They use these more than their beak for fighting. They lie on their backs and lash out with these talons.

The cassowary of New Guinea and Australia is the only bird which can kill a man. It strikes hard with the long claw on each foot.

Self Defence

Some birds, like hawks, falcons, eagles and owls fight to defend themselves. They usually fall on their backs to strike at an enemy with talons and beak.

Some of the larger birds that are not birds of prey but have powerful beaks, will also fight. Herons stab upwards with beaks like daggers.

Most birds fly away rather than stand and fight. Sometimes small birds will fight each other in a fit of bad temper. Sparrows and starlings do, but not very often.

Why Do Birds Fight?

Most fighting between birds is about territory during the breeding season. These fights are not usually very fierce. They are more a matter of bluff. When a male bird enters another bird's territory, the owner becomes aggressive. This means he looks ready for a fight. He fluffs out his feathers so that he looks extra big, and shows any coloured patches in his plumage. He pushes his beak forward as if ready to peck. Usually this is enough to make the other male fly away. The aggressive display is more bluff than anything else. Even if it comes to a fight birds do not usually cause serious injury to each other.

Skuas are sea birds which kill other birds. When nesting they will attack a man, who must wear a steel helmet.

Bird Language

Birds make many sounds besides the well-known bird song. They have special calls for food, courtship and help.

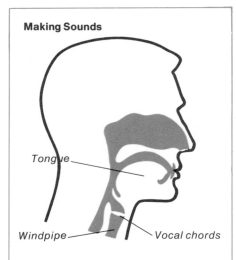

Making Sounds

Tongue

Windpipe — *Vocal chords*

The human voice box is high up in the throat. People use the air they breathe out when they speak. The air passes between the vocal chords. These vibrate to produce a sound. This sound can be changed by the way the lips, cheeks, tongue and teeth are moved.

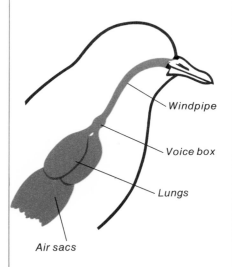

Windpipe

Voice box

Lungs

Air sacs

A bird's voice box is low in the throat and has no vocal chords. Instead, it has lots of tiny muscles which alter its shape. All the sounds a bird makes come from deep down in the voice box. A bird does not use its tongue or cheeks to shape the sounds, and it has no teeth.

The nightingale is only $6\frac{1}{2}$ inches (165 mm.) long. It is famous all over the world for its lovely song. It sings during the day but also at night, when most other birds are asleep.

Bird Song

Birds make many sorts of sounds. The best known sound is bird song. Usually, the male birds sing, for two reasons. One is to warn other birds to keep out of their territory.

The other reason is to attract a female, so that they can mate, build a nest, and bring up a family.

Size and Sound

The biggest birds do not necessarily sing loudest or best. A wren, only about four inches (102 mm.) long, pours out a torrent of song, loud and sweet. Some of the largest birds, such as the ostrich, which is eight feet (2.4 m.) high, sing no song at all.

Bird Calls

Birds make other sounds besides song. They are known as calls. One is the alarm call. One bird uses this call to tell the others that danger is near.

Some birds have a special call when they have found food. They make this call to guide the other birds to the food.

Birds that are courting sometimes make very unusual sounds.

Another kind of call is the call for help. If a bird is trapped or helpless, it screams for help. Young birds also call out to tell their parents when they are hungry.

Call to Food

Gulls feed on many kinds of food. They have special calls which tell other gulls that they have found something to eat. Gulls eat a lot of fish. They make a special call when a shoal of small fishes comes to the surface. Other gulls far away hear the special call and come flying over to share the food.

Gulls also feed on odds and ends, like bits of bread. When there is plenty of this sort of food around, the gulls gather just at the sight of the food.

In this way, other gulls always know what sort of food is available.

Love Call

When birds are courting they often sing to their mates. Some birds make music in other ways. The woodpecker pecks rapidly at the branch or trunk of a tree. In this way it makes a drumming sound. This is the woodpecker's love call. Drumming has been most studied in the greater spotted woodpecker, but the green woodpecker shown here has also been known to drum.

Other birds have different mating calls. One bird sings with its tail. This is the snipe. When courting, the male snipe flies up high and then dives. As he does this, he twists and turns and holds out some of his tail feathers. The air rushing through these tail feathers makes a bleating sound. This noise is the snipe's love call to its mate.

Call for Help

Glass cage

Wall

Chick calling for help

Mother hen

Chick calling for help

A hen with a brood of little chicks walks around clucking. The chicks hear her and cheep back. So the chicks always know where their mother is, and she always knows where her chicks are.

If a chick gets lost, it cheeps more loudly and the hen looks round for it. If she cannot see it, she will keep on looking until she finds her chick.

If a chick is put inside a glass dome, the hen can see the chick, but she cannot hear it. So she will take no notice of the chick, even though he is calling for help, because she cannot hear the cry.

If another chick is hidden behind a wall, it will call to its mother for help. She will go and look for it, because she can hear it, even though she cannot see it. She knows by listening to the call that the chick needs her.

Colours of Birds

The colours of a bird's plumage are useful in several ways— as camouflage, as a warning, and for courtship display.

Blue-crowned pigeon

Scarlet macaw

Using Colour
Birds' colours have many uses. They can serve as camouflage, and they can also be used as a warning to rivals during courtship. Birds of the same kind recognise each other by their colours. Bright colours are used in courtship to attract the hens.

Different Colours
Owls and nightjars come out at night, and have dull colours. Birds living in cold places where there is a lot of snow are mainly white. They are not easily seen against the snow. Birds in hot countries are usually very brightly coloured. This does not mean that they are easily seen. The flowers and trees where they live are also brightly coloured, so the birds are well camouflaged.

Macaws live in Tropical America. They are very brightly coloured birds, and belong to the parrot family. All parrots live in hot countries and most of them are brightly coloured. The scarlet macaw is about three feet (914 mm.) long. It has a powerful beak and can crack hard nuts.

The blue-crowned pigeon is another brightly coloured bird. It lives in New Guinea. The blue-crowned pigeons are the giants of the pigeon family. They are nearly three feet (914 mm.) long. They feed on the ground but fly into trees when in danger.

The robin redbreast uses its breast as a warning to rivals. When about to attack, he points his bill at the sky and shows off his breast.

When a buzzard soars, the marks under its wings are like the recognition marks on a warplane.

Sand grouse chicks are well camouflaged. Their backs are a sandy colour, broken up into jigsaw patches by yellow lines.

Snowy owls live in the Arctic where there is a lot of snow. Their white plumage hides them from the animals they hunt. The white feathers have another very important function—they stop heat leaving the body, so that the bird keeps warm in a cold climate.

A penguin has a black back and a white front. When the penguin swims, its white front blends with the sky when an enemy looks up from below. The black back blends with the dark sea below when an enemy is flying overhead.

The frigate bird courts a female by inflating the red sac under its chin, and then spreading its wings.

Migration and Geography

Birds migrate from one part of the world to another in search of plentiful food. Many birds travel a long way every year.

The Seasons

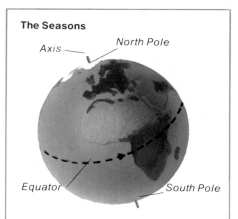

The earth is round. Imagine a line running through its centre from the the North Pole to the South Pole. This is the earth's axis. Imagine another line running round the centre separating the Northern Hemisphere from the Southern Hemisphere. This line is the Equator.

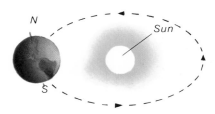

The earth moves round the sun in 365 days, which is one year. The earth is slightly slanted on its axis, so sometimes the south is nearer the sun than the north. Then it is summer in the south.

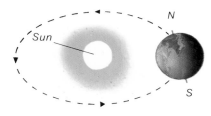

When the north is nearest the sun it is summer in the north, and winter in the Southern Hemisphere. It is the changing length of day which tells the birds it is time to migrate.

Swallows gather on overhead wires to migrate together. They nest in the Northern Hemisphere, and fly south just before the winter.

Migration

A lot of birds fly from one part of the world to another and back. They go from a place where food is getting scarce to a place where food is plentiful. This is called migration. The birds fly away to find food at the time when they build their nests and lay their eggs. They make sure the young birds will not go without food.

Swallows

Swallows live in South Africa, but when winter comes there they fly north to Europe where the summer is just beginning. They go back at the end of the northern summer to South Africa, where the southern summer is just beginning. Swallows must do this because they feed on flying insects, which are very scarce in winter.

Other birds migrate to avoid the winter, when the ground is frozen over, and there are no seeds or insects for them to eat.

When and Where

Birds start to migrate when the days shorten, and winter is coming. They fly away to warmer places. Each year, they follow regular routes, called flyways. Some birds fly a short distance, others go a long way. Birds travel in large flocks to protect themselves from enemies.

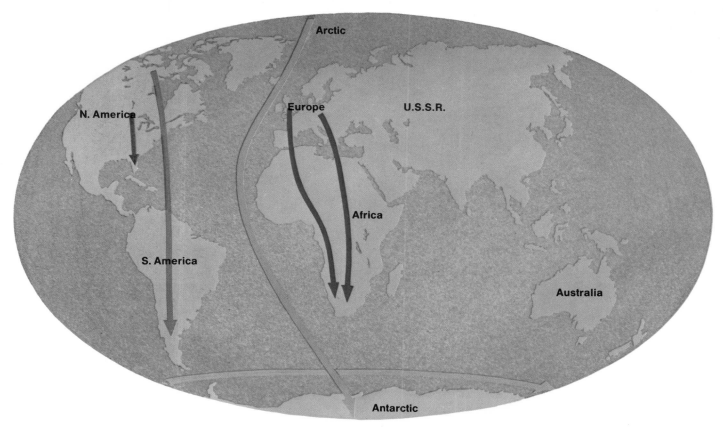

 **Ruby-throated hummingbird**

 **Golden plover**

The American golden plover, nine inches (229 mm.) long, flies from the Arctic to southern South America 9,000 miles (14,484 km.) away.

The ruby-throated hummingbird, three inches (76 mm.) long, nests in southern Canada and flies 1,500 miles (2,414 km.) to

 Arctic tern

Florida for the winter.

The arctic tern, 15 inches (381 mm.) long, flies from the Arctic to the Antarctic each year, a distance of 11,000 miles (17,703 km.) each way.

Swallows, six inches (152 mm.) long, fly 6,000 miles (9,656 km.) from Europe to

 Swallow

 Wandering albatross

South Africa.

The wandering albatross, 4½ feet (1·4 m.) long, nests on Antarctic islands, and spends the rest of the year flying 10,000 miles (16,093 km.) or more over the Southern Ocean.

When birds migrate, they often fly in large flocks for safety.

Some birds fly in formation when they migrate.

These migrating geese are flying in a V-shaped formation.

Finding the Way

Migrating birds know when to fly away, but they also know where to fly and how to get there. They use the sun, moon and stars.

American robin

Blue jay

Some birds migrate by day, like these two. They use the sun to find their way, just as sailors did in the days before there were compasses.

Birds ready to migrate face in the direction they have to go, if they are placed in a large glass cage with the sun shining.

If the sky is cloudy, without even a small blue patch, the birds often face all directions in a cage. They are lost, because they cannot see the sun.

Which Direction?
When birds migrate, they have to find their way from one place to another place a long way away. They find their way by using the sun, stars and moon. This is called celestial navigation.

Cloudy Skies
When thick clouds blot out the sky, the birds lose sight of the sun, stars or moon. They lose their way. When the clouds or fog clear, the birds can get back on the correct course.

Cuckoos
Young birds can migrate without their parents to show them the way by using the sun to navigate. Baby cuckoos never see their real parents. The parents lay their eggs in Europe (in other birds' nests) and then fly back to Africa. A month later, the young cuckoos fly to Africa. They have never been that way before, but they use the sun as a guide.

Travelling
Birds usually fly at a height of about 4,000 feet (about 1,200 m.) for about 50 miles (about 80 km.). Then they stop to rest and feed. During one day they travel perhaps 500 miles (about 800 km.). The American golden plover is unusual. It flies 2,000 miles (about 3,200 km.) without stopping.

Pigeons have been used to carry messages for thousands of years. They have to be taught to come back to the place they started from. At first they travel only short distances, but later they manage to return from far away.

Rose-breasted grosbeak

Great-crested flycatcher

Scientists know birds use the stars to navigate. They put birds in a planetarium, which is a dome with a picture of the night sky on it. The birds face the way they have to migrate. When the dome is moved round the birds move round, too.

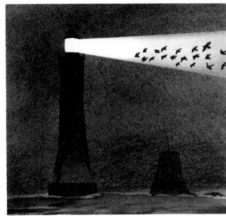

On foggy nights, migrating birds often crash into lighthouses. Many are killed. They have lost their way because they cannot see the stars. They are attracted by the light from the lighthouse.

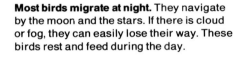

Most birds migrate at night. They navigate by the moon and the stars. If there is cloud or fog, they can easily lose their way. These birds rest and feed during the day.

Watching the moon through a telescope to see the birds against the moon was one way of studying migration. This needed a lot of patience, and was not very accurate.

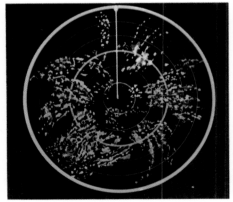

Today, people watch a radar screen in comfort. This tells them the direction the birds are going, and how many birds are passing across the screen.

Banding, or ringing, is another way of studying migration. A metal band is put on the leg of a bird about to migrate. When other people find the bird, they can trace its flight path

Birds in Groups

Most birds live together for safety's sake, and also to make sure that as many eyes as possible are on the lookout for food.

Nest made of palm fronds

Village weavers live in equatorial Africa. They build their nests in palm trees, and there are many nests to a tree. The weavers strip palm fronds from the tree to make their nests. This may eventually kill the tree.

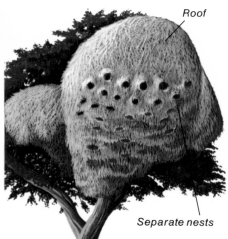

Roof

Separate nests

The social weavers of Africa are the size of a sparrow. They build tenement nests. Many pairs of them build a roof of grass and straw. Then each pair builds its own nest under it.

Company
Some birds live almost entirely on their own, and come together only in the breeding season. They are called solitary birds. Most birds prefer company. They live in pairs, or small groups, large flocks or colonies.

Food
One advantage of living together is that there is more than just one pair of eyes looking for food.

Enemies
Another advantage is that there is more than one pair of eyes looking out for enemies. If one bird in a flock sees an enemy coming it takes off. The others see it and then do the same.

Some birds even give an alarm call as they fly off. This is an even better warning to the other birds that danger is near.

Breeding Colonies
Flocks often break up when the nesting season begins, and each pair of birds nests on its own. Some birds nest together, and this is called a breeding colony. There is great safety in a breeding colony. If an enemy is sighted, all the parents come together and scream or peck to try to frighten the enemy away. Birds which breed in colonies usually never nest on their own.

Penguins live in colonies. When it is very cold, they sometimes huddle together to keep warm. At breeding time, a colony of penguins may contain millions.

Hawk

Flock of starlings

Starlings fly about in loose flocks. If a hawk flies near them, they form a box shape for safety, until the hawk has left their territory.

Flamingos live in huge colonies on large lakes. They form large colourful groups.

If anything disturbs the flamingos, they all take off together.

They fly round and land together. Flamingos also nest together.

Curious Behaviour

Many birds do some very strange things. Some of these are easily explained, others are still a mystery.

The Pecking Order

A

B

C

Not many years ago, scientists noticed a curious behaviour among domestic hens. Everybody knew they pecked each other. Then scientists saw that there was a boss hen (A) which pecked all the others but was never pecked back. B never pecked A but pecked all the rest. C never pecked A or B but pecked all the rest. And so it went on, down to the last hen. She was pecked by all of them, and had last choice of food.

Strange but Simple

Many things which birds do look odd at first. A lot of these strange actions have very simple explanations. For example, when birds strut around, or show off their feathers, they are trying to court a female, or perhaps warning off another bird.

Odd Habits

Birds do sometimes do things which puzzle even the best experts. Anting, for example, is a very strange thing to do. Why do birds pick up ants and rub them on their wing feathers?

Blue tits also have odd habits. They sometimes peck away the putty from around a window pane. People once thought they were doing this to look for insects and spiders in the cracks of the putty. Then people thought perhaps the birds wanted to eat the oil in the putty. Blue tits will also come inside a house and peck at wallpaper, or the backs of books. Nobody can say for certain why they do this.

Songbirds will, very rarely, pick up an ant in the beak and rub it under their wing feathers. They repeat this several times. People have suggested that they might be using acid from the ant to clean their feathers, but no-one knows for certain.

The lapwing gets up and runs away when an enemy goes near its nest. She does not run fast and she drags one wing as if it were broken. The enemy thinks she is hurt, and follows her, leaving the nest unharmed. Then suddenly she flies off.

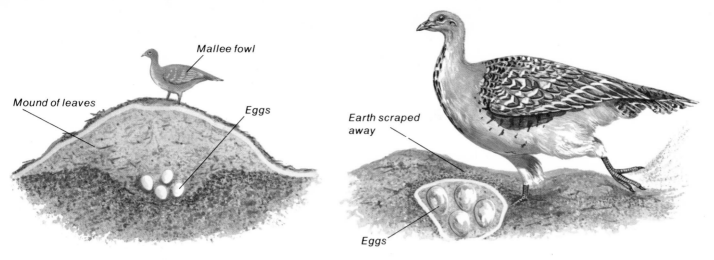

Mallee fowl

Mound of leaves

Eggs

Earth scraped away

Eggs

Australian mallee fowl build a huge mound of dry leaves in which to lay their eggs. The mound acts as an incubator for the eggs.

The cock mallee fowl uses his tongue as a thermometer. When the nest gets too hot, he opens the mound up by moving some of the leaves, so that the eggs can cool down. When the nest gets too cold, he covers it up again to warm up the eggs.

Swifts are known to sleep on the wing. They hardly ever land. Even when they are nesting they spend most of their time in the air, hunting and sleeping.

Jays bury acorns. In winter they come and find them, to eat them. They can go straight to each acorn. The puzzle is how they know where the acorns are.

Everybody once thought birds never hibernated. Then, 20 years ago, a poorwill was found hibernating in the Colorado desert. Nobody knows why.

Magpies steal rings, coins and pieces of metal or glass. If they can, they carry them away and hide them. They are attracted by bright objects, but no-one knows why.

How Birds Die

Many birds die very young. They are killed by accidents, starvation, or by enemies that hunt them.

The peregrine falcon is one of the winged enemies of birds. He attacks other birds from the sky. He strikes with his talons at the unlucky prey.

Peregrine falcon

Pheasant

Small birds with eyes on the sides of the head cannot see very well straight in front. Sometimes they fly into things.

A cat can creep up and pounce on young birds. They are not used to watching for danger and do not fly off quickly.

Young birds only just learning to fly sometimes lose their balance and fall. They cannot fly up, and die on the ground of starvation, or are eaten.

Accidents

Many birds are killed by accidents. Often they die very young. A brood of ducklings, for example, might all die before they grow up. The mother might accidentally tread on one, a crow could kill another. The duck might sit on one in the water and drown it by accident. A rat could kill one more. Another duckling might fall sick and die. Perhaps only one of the ducklings will grow up.

Young Birds

Three or four young birds out of every five die during the first three to six months after hatching. They may be killed by enemies, or fall ill and die, or their mothers may neglect them. The weather may be too cold, or too wet for them to survive. They may also crash when learning to fly.

Where do Sick Birds Go?

Dead birds are seldom seen except perhaps on the roads, where they have been killed by the traffic. Sick birds try to find holes and corners to creep into, and there they die.

Cold Weather

Hard winters kill many birds. They do not mind the cold when they have plenty to eat. When the ground is iced over they cannot get either seeds or insects, and they cannot drink.

The Threat of Pollution

Pollution is man-made. Many substances used today are harmful in the quantities in which some of them are used and thrown away.

Dead and dying seabirds are sometimes found washed up on the shore covered in

With skill and patience, experts sometimes manage to clean birds up. When birds are covered with oil, they are unable to fly or swim, and so they cannot catch food to keep themselves alive.

oil. Sometimes they can be saved, but often there is nothing anyone can do to help

Today's Problem

Pollution means making something impure. The world's land, air and water is becoming polluted with man-made substances.

A few years ago, hardly anyone mentioned pollution. Now many people are talking about it, and taking action to stop it. Pollution has become a great threat to animals and humans alike.

Oil

When oil is pumped from a ship into the sea, it pollutes the water. The oil also coats the feathers of sea birds, and they cannot fly or swim properly. They often starve to death.

them. They are the victims of oil pollution in the sea.

Chemicals

Another kind of pollution comes from the land. Chemicals called pesticides are used to kill weed and insect pests. Insects which have been killed by pesticides are sometimes eaten by small birds or by fishes. These animals are then often eaten by bigger animals. The bigger animals are harmed by the chemicals in the food they have eaten.

This happens to the osprey, a fish-eating eagle. If ospreys eat fish which have fed on polluted insects, they either lay no eggs, or the eggs which they lay never hatch. So the osprey future is in danger from pollution.

Legend and History

Birds are often found in legends and folklore. They have sometimes played a part in the world's history, too.

Phoenix

Stork

Dove

Pelican

Geese

Birds as National Emblems

Kiwi
(New Zealand)

Bald eagle
(United States)

Quetzel
(Guatemala)

Myths and Legends

The phoenix was a mythical bird. It never existed, but many wonderful tales were told about it. The phoenix was believed to appear once every 500 years. It was said to build a nest, set the nest on fire, and then perish in the flames, to grow again from the ashes three days later.

Symbols

Many birds are used as symbols, to represent something important. The white dove is perhaps the most famous symbol. It stands for peace.

After the biblical flood, Noah sent out a dove from the ark. to find out if the waters had gone down. Ever since then, a dove has meant peace, and a sign of good things to come. The truth is that the dove is one of the most quarrelsome of birds.

The pelican is a symbol of piety. People used to believe that the female pelican pecked her own breast to feed her chicks on her own blood.

The stork was said to bring good luck. People also used to say that a stork brought a new baby, carrying it in its beak.

Geese

The geese of Rome once saved the city from invaders. Their cackling woke the city as the invaders tried to take Rome by surprise.

Facts and Figures

Largest land bird (flightless):
The ostrich measures up to nine feet (2.7 m.) tall to the top of its head, and weighs up to 345 lb. (156 kg.).

Heaviest flying bird:
The mute swan is one of the heaviest flying birds, weighing sometimes over $50\frac{1}{2}$ lb. (23 kg.).

Smallest flying bird:
The bee hummingbird measures only $2\frac{1}{4}$ inches (57 mm.) long, and weighs only $\frac{1}{16}$ ounce (1.8 g.).

Greatest wing span:
The marabou stork has been known to have a wing span, tip to tip, of twelve feet (3.7 m.). The wandering albatross has a maximum wing span of $11\frac{1}{2}$ ft. (3.5 m.).

Longest migration:
Arctic terns fly 22,000 miles (34,400 km.) from the Arctic to the Antarctic and back again each year.

Fastest speeds in the air:
On the level: spine-tailed swift, over 100 m.p.h. (161 k.p.h.); the racing pigeon can reach speeds of 94.3 m.p.h. (152 k.p.h.). The loon has clocked up 90 m.p.h. (145 k.p.h.), and the lammergeier vulture 79.5 m.p.h. (128 k.p.h.); in a dive: peregrine falcon reaches speeds of 180 m.p.h. (290 k.p.h.) when stooping, which means diving on prey.

Fastest speeds on land:
The ostrich has been known to reach a speed of 37 m.p.h. (60 k.p.h.), and possibly more. A month-old ostrich chick can run at 35 m.p.h. (56 k.p.h.).

Fastest speeds under water:
The gentoo penguin can reach a speed of 22 m.p.h. (35 k.p.h.) under water.

Greatest heights flown:
The Egyptian goose is thought to have flown at a height of 35,000 feet (10,668 m.). A chough has been seen on Mount Everest at a height of over 26,000 feet (7,924 m.). A species of small bird was also recorded on radar as reaching a height of 21,000 feet (6,400 m.) when on migration.

Fastest wing beats:
The hummingbird's wings beat at a speed of 200 beats a second when it is hovering.

Greatest number of wing beats:
The golden plover flies 2,000 miles (3,218 km.) on migration, taking 35 hours. It makes two wing beats a second. So on the journey it makes 252,000 wing beats.

Greatest depth reached by diving bird:
A loon has been known to reach a depth of 240 feet (73 m.).

Longest stay under water:
The Adélie penguin can stay under water for three minutes, and possibly up to five minutes.

Largest egg:
An ostrich egg can measure up to eight inches (203 mm.) long, and weighs over 31 lb. (14 kg.).

Smallest egg:
The bee hummingbird lays the smallest egg. It measures $\frac{3}{16}$ inch (4.5 mm.) and weighs $\frac{5}{1000}$ ounce (0.14 g.).

Largest clutch of eggs:
A mallard duck has been known to lay 16 eggs. The mallard will lay up to a hundred eggs, if the eggs are taken away as soon as they are laid. A domestic hen laid 351 eggs in a year, and another laid 1,515 in 8 years, but the laying dropped off with age.

Longest nesting season:
The mallee fowl's nesting season is eleven months long.

Commonest bird:
The starling is the commonest bird in the world, apart from the domesticated chicken. The common starling is found all over Europe, most of Asia, and has also been introduced into North America, Australia and New Zealand.

Rarest bird:
It is very difficult to say which bird is the rarest. Probably it is the noisy scrub bird of Australia, thought to be extinct, and rediscovered in 1961.

Longest lived bird:
In captivity: the eagle owl has reached the age of 68 years.
In the wild: a herring gull has been known to have lived until 32 years old. Records of nearly 100 years for cockatoos are unreliable.

Longest time airborne:
Swifts spend most of their lives in the air. Even when they are nesting, they still spend half their time on the wing. They sleep in the air, too. From the time they learn to fly, swifts may never land again until they build a nest. This could be as long as 21 months.

Biggest pest:
The dioch of Africa is possibly the biggest bird pest. There are millions of them, and they feed on grains. They are therefore a menace to farmers. Trees are sometimes smashed under the weight of diochs which land on the branches. A small tree holds as many as 500 nests, and a large one 6,000 nests. The dioch is possibly the most numerous species of bird in the world. There are as many as 500,000 nests over an area of 125 acres (50 ha.). Over an area of 5,000 acres (2,000 ha.), there could be as many as 200 million nests.

Species of birds:
There are over 8,000 species of birds. In 1962, the count was 8,580 species. The insect world has many more species than birds, probably somewhere between two million and ten million, it is impossible to be accurate.

Nests:
The simplest nest is no nest at all. The king and emperor penguins keep their eggs warm on their feet. The cuckoo does not build a nest. It lays its eggs in other birds' nests.
The long-tailed tit builds a nest five or six inches high (127 or 152 mm.), and the hollow inside is about three inches across (76 mm.). The nest will hold two parent birds about $5\frac{1}{2}$ inches (140 mm.) long, including a three-inch (76 mm.) tail, and also up to twelve fledglings. The nest is made of moss, cobwebs, hair and lichens, and is

Facts and Figures

lined with 2,000 or more feathers. The nest takes two to three days to complete. A lot of this time is taken up by collecting the material.

Pigeons, on the other hand, do not take as much trouble as tits. They build a very rough nest, and looking at the nest from underneath, the eggs can be seen through the nest.

Crows have been known to use telegraph wires to make a nest. Once, in South Africa, the linesmen putting up the wires noticed that the crows were picking up the cut-off ends of wire. They wove these into a nest shape.

Blackbirds have been known to weave yards of expensive lace they have stolen into a nest.

European wrens will roost in a clump when the weather is very bad. They go into a hole or a nest box. There can be up to three tiers of wrens in a small nest box. As many as 52 have been counted in one box at once.

Storks often build nests on the tops of houses. It was thought to be a sign of good luck to have a stork nest on the roof. People sometimes build platforms on their roofs to make it easy for the storks to nest there, and bring good luck.

The smallest nest is that of the hummingbird. It measures $\frac{4}{5}$ inch (20 mm.) across, and about one inch (25 mm.) high.

Feeding:
Small birds, such as tits, feed their broods on caterpillars. During the time they feed their young, they collect as many as 10,000 caterpillars.

Incubation periods:
The incubation period is the time taken for a bird to develop before hatching out. Here are some figures for the length of incubation for different birds:
small birds: two weeks
wandering albatross: 73 days
kiwi: 80 days
royal albatross: 81 days

Fledging periods:
The fledging period is the time taken for a baby bird to grow its proper feathers, after shedding its down. Here are some figures for the fledging

periods of different birds:
small birds: two weeks
pigeons, nightjars, hummingbirds, woodpeckers: four weeks
bustards, owls and crows: five weeks
smaller albatross: 20-21 weeks
Californian condor: 26-30 weeks
emperor penguin: 35-39 weeks
wandering albatross: as much as 44-45 weeks
king penguin: up to 56 weeks. Sometimes food is scarce, and the baby is not fed. This is why it takes so long for the young chick to leave its parents. It does not grow if it is not fed.

Threatened Species
Well over a hundred different kinds of birds are today threatened with extinction. That is to say, their numbers are so low that an unusual event could wipe out the last of them. Many of them live on small oceanic islands, where they are being crowded out by domestic animals or people. Others, through hunting or because their habitat has been changed, by farming, for example, are driven to live in a small area. There are others that belong to species which have grown old. Species, like people, age and die. A species now old may have ranged over a whole continent once. Gradually its numbers have declined until only a few are left.

When there are a few animals of one species left a natural catastrophe may wipe out the survivors. It may be a typhoon, hurricane, earthquake, or a prolonged cold winter. Or it may be an animal introduced from another country which preys on them. Sometimes the forest in which they live is cut down, the land is ploughed, an airfield built. Or it may be they are over-hunted. So the last remnant disappears.

Here are a few of the threatened species and why they are in danger:

Californian condor, *Gymnogyps californianus*
An old species, this vulture is nine feet across the wings. Its bones are dug up all over the southern United States. These bones come from birds

that died 3,000 to 10,000 years ago. During this century the vulture has been shot and poisoned. Now there are only about 50 left.

Everglade kite, *Rostrhamus sociabilis plumbeus*
This kite feeds on the giant freshwater snails in the Everglade swamps. There are less than a dozen left. This is because its nests are raided by other birds, especially grackles. Also, people visiting the swamps often disturb the kites when they are nesting.

Galapagos hawk, *Buteo galapagoensis*
There are only about 200 of this hawk —it is really a buzzard—on the Galapagos Islands in the Pacific Ocean. They are shot because they steal chickens. Also goats destroy the vegetation which the hawks eat, and as the number of people rises, so do the numbers of goats.

Monkey-eating eagle, *Pithecophaga jefferyi*
This magnificent eagle is much in demand for zoos. It is also fashionable in the Philippines, where it lives, to have a stuffed eagle in the house (a status symbol). Dead or alive the eagle fetches a high price. There are only a hundred left.

Whooping crane, *Grus americana*
This is another species dying of old age. There are only about 50 left. It nests in western Canada and migrates for the winter to Texas. It used to be shot in Canada and Texas and also all along its migration route. Now it is protected everywhere, in the hope of saving it.

Eskimo curlew, *Numenius borealis*
Centuries ago flocks of Eskimo curlew nested in the Canadian arctic. Each year they would migrate down the east coast of North America, to South America. In the spring the flocks would fly north again, up the Mississippi Valley. Everywhere they were shot at, especially on migration, so that only one or a few from each flock would get through. No eggs of

this curlew have been seen for the last 30 years. So they must have a nesting ground that nobody has yet found.

New Zealand laughing owl, *Sceloglaux albafacies*

This owl used to live in all parts of New Zealand and also on other South Pacific Islands. It was known to the Maoris and the early British settlers. Gradually its numbers fell. First it disappeared from North Island, then from South Island. The last one was seen in 1914. It was a dying species finally killed off by stoats taken to New Zealand. It could be called extinct except that every now and then naturalists report hearing its laughing call.

Ivory-billed woodpecker, *Campephilus principalis*

This is one of the largest and most handsome of all woodpeckers. Its feathers are black, white and scarlet. Its bill looks like ivory. Each pair needs 2,000 acres (800 ha.) of forest, with old dead trees to feed themselves and their babies on insect grubs. Gradually, the forests in the south-eastern United States and Cuba, where the woodpecker lived, were cut down. It was thought to be extinct. Then three were seen in 1960 and 1961, and another in 1963. In 1966, five more were seen. Some of the forest trees are being left in the hope that it will survive.

Birds Rediscovered

Takahe, *Notornis mantelli*

In the early 19th century, bones of what was thought to be an extinct bird were dug up at several places in New Zealand. From time to time, between 1849 and 1949, skins or dead birds were found, which were exactly like the "fossil". In 1949 an expedition found a colony of takahes living among the tussock grass 3,000 feet (914 m.) high on Murchison Mountains in South Island. There were 200 to 300. The colony is now a reserve.

Noisy scrub bird, *Atrichornis clamosus*

This was a bird in Western Australia that made so much noise it got on people's nerves. It was unknown until 1843 and had died out by 1889. This was because the scrub in which it lived was cleared. One man claimed to have heard the bird in 1920. Then one was seen in 1961. A park of 13,500 acres has been set up around that spot and there are probably 80-100 noisy scrub birds living in it now.

Glossary of Terms

Bird: warm-blooded animal with its body covered with feathers.

Flying: moving through the air by beating wings. This is powered flight.

Gliding: moving through the air with fixed wings and with no driving force.

Hovering: to hang suspended in the air over one spot with small beats of the wings.

Primary feathers: the long feathers in the outer half of a bird's wings.

Plumage: all the feathers on a bird's body.

Train: the extra long tail found in birds such as peacocks and pheasants. The train of a peacock strictly speaking is made up of long feathers just in front of the tail feathers.

Down: small soft feathers covering a baby bird. Many birds have an undercoat of down throughout their lives.

Gape: beak wide open showing the throat.

Crop: thin-walled bag of skin opening into the gullet and used for storing food. Found in many birds especially grain eaters.

Gizzard: a bird's stomach. It has thick walls of muscle and is used to grind up food.

Air-sacs: bags of thin skin leading out of the lungs of birds into the body, even into the bones.

Breeding season: the time of year in which birds mark out territories, build nests, lay their eggs and rear their young.

Incubating: keeping an egg warm so that it can develop, usually by a parent sitting on it.

Hatching: when a baby bird pecks its way out of the shell the egg is said to hatch and the chick to hatch out.

Brood: the baby birds hatched from a single clutch of eggs.

Brood patch: bald spot on the breast of a bird which develops when there are eggs to be incubated.

Clutch: a complete set of eggs laid by one female and all brooded at the same time.

Fledgling: a young bird that has got its first complete set of feathers.

Flock: a gathering of birds.

Song post: a particular perch used by a bird for singing, especially one used to advertise a territory.

Territory: an area defended by a bird or other animal in which it has its home or nest.

Aggression: threatening behaviour sometimes leading to an attack.

Pecking order: a social system in which each member of a flock or herd holds a definite rank which is decided by intermittent fighting or pecking.

Camouflage: disguising something by means of colours.

Migration: going from one place to another usually from a feeding to a nesting area and back.

Evolution: the process of change. In living things, the changes cause new species to come into being.

How to Watch Birds

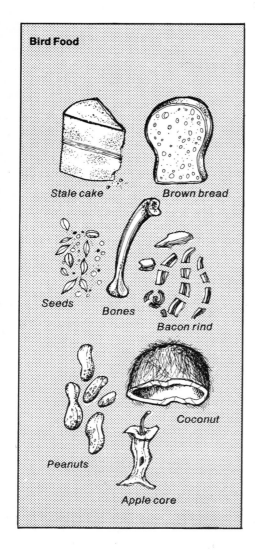

Bird Food

Stale cake

Brown bread

Seeds

Bones

Bacon rind

Coconut

Peanuts

Apple core

Looking for Birds

Bird-watching is a very rewarding hobby, because birds can be seen everywhere. There is no need to go far to look for birds. You can start at home. Use your house as a ready-made hide for watching birds. Attract more birds by putting out food and water.

Food

You can put food on the ground, on a window ledge, or better still, on a bird table, which you can make yourself (see page 56). The water, for drinking and bathing, should be in a shallow dish or tray on the ground.

Identifying Birds

Can you identify all the birds you see? If you see a bird you do not know, make a note of its colours in a notebook. Describe its size. Say whether the bird has any white patches or bands of colour on its

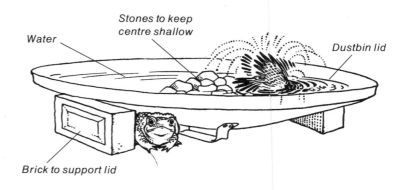

Water

Stones to keep centre shallow

Dustbin lid

Brick to support lid

An old, upturned dustbin lid makes a good bird bath. Support it with bricks or stones. If it is deep in the middle, put in some stones. Then watch the birds come to bathe. Any shallow container will do for a bird bath.

If you have a garden, you could dig a small pond, and line it with polythene. Make sure that at least one side of the pond slopes gently, so that the birds can get in easily.

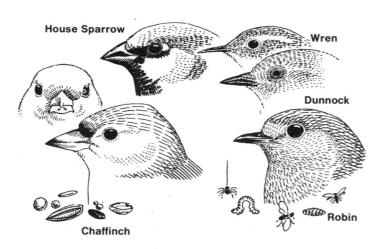

House Sparrow

Wren

Dunnock

Robin

Chaffinch

Always look carefully at a bird's beak. It is often an aid to identification—and may tell you about the bird's food, too. Short, stubby beaks are typical of birds which are mainly seed-eaters (like the house sparrow and chaffinch on the left), while pointed beaks are typical of birds which are mainly insect-eaters (wren, dunnock and robin).

Some birds have special shapes of beaks for their particular needs. For instance, herons have long, dagger-like beaks for striking fish, snipe have long, thin beaks for probing in mud, and owls have hooked beaks for tearing flesh.

head, wings or tail. Also, look carefully at the shape of its bill and note what it is eating. Often, birds which eat mainly seeds have short, stubby beaks, and birds which eat mainly insects have sharp, pointed beaks.

Identification

Draw a rough sketch of the bird, showing the shape of the beak and the tail, and what the main colours are. Then look the bird up in an identification book. *The Observer's Book of Birds* (published by Warne) is a useful book for beginners. *The Field Guide to the Birds of Britain and Europe* (published by Collins) is useful for more experienced bird-watchers. Keep a list of all the birds you see, and always be on the look-out for a 'new' bird. Join the *Young Ornithologists' Club*, The Lodge, Sandy, Bedfordshire, to further your interest.

Once you have got to know the birds near your home, then you are ready to go further afield. You need not go very far. Even if you live in a town, there is probably a good place nearby—a park, river or reservoir.

Equipment

One great thing about bird-watching is that you do not need much equipment. If you are seriously interested in bird-watching, however, a pair of binoculars is useful. It is often very difficult to get very close to birds without frightening them away. Binoculars help you to see a bird clearly from a distance.

A large-scale map is also useful. Firstly it will show you the good places to go to watch birds, and secondly, it will show you how to get there.

Cover

Try to hide yourself as much as possible when you watch birds. Use trees or hedges as a cover. If you are watching one place, like a pond, for some time, you could put up a screen of branches to hide yourself. You could even make a hide, or little tent, out of four poles and a piece of canvas.

Habitat

Note down all the birds you see, and in what habitat you see them. The habitat is the type of country or surroundings in which a bird lives. Here is a list of habitats: woods, farmland, mountain and moorland, rivers and marshes, lakes and gravel pits, seashore and estuaries, cliffs and sea, and parks and gardens.

Keep lists on all your outings, and you will find that some birds are seen only in one sort of habitat; others in several. Soon, you will be able to forecast what birds you are likely to see before you visit somewhere new, and you will be able to notice new or rare birds.

Binoculars are helpful if you are very interested in birds, although you can still enjoy bird-watching without them. 8 × 30 binoculars are suitable for beginners. They magnify eight times.

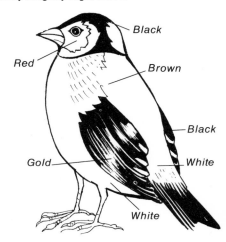

Draw a picture of any bird you do not recognise. Note the shape of its beak, and the colours of its plumage. Later on, you can look the bird up in an identification book.

Date	Time	Name of Bird	Food Eaten	Drink	Bathe

Keep a list of all the birds you see. Make a note of the time you see them, and their names. Say what sort of food they eat, and whether they drink or bathe. In this way, you will soon learn how different birds behave.

Making a Nest Box

For metric conversion of the measurements given here, please refer to Index.

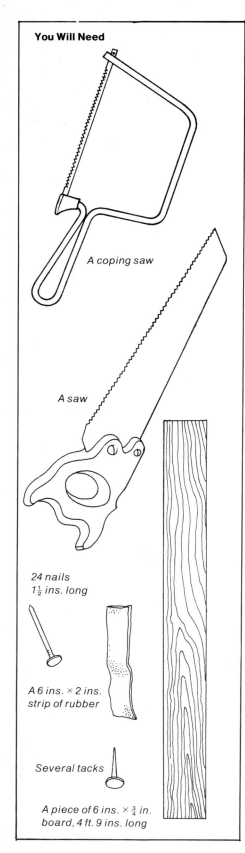

You Will Need

A coping saw

A saw

24 nails 1½ ins. long

A 6 ins. × 2 ins. strip of rubber

Several tacks

A piece of 6 ins. × ¾ in. board, 4 ft. 9 ins. long

This is an inexpensive do-it-yourself nest box, which you can make even if you have very little skill, and only a few tools. It will attract blue tits, great tits, and even nuthatches. If birds come to nest in your nest box, make sure that you do not disturb them. Then you will be able to watch the birds as they bring up their young.

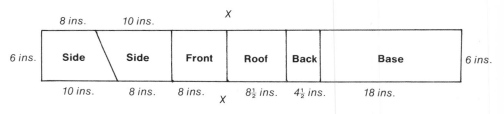

	X						
6 ins.	Side	Side	Front	Roof	Back	Base	6 ins.

8 ins.   10 ins.

10 ins.   8 ins.   8 ins.   8½ ins.   4½ ins.   18 ins.

X

Fig. 1

The large piece of unplaned wood provides all the main pieces of the nest box. Measure the wood off as shown here. Use a sharp pencil to mark off the lengths. The exact length of the back does not matter, as the pieces left top and bottom are only used for attaching the nest box to a tree or post. Note the line XX in the diagram. You should make a special sloping cut here where the front and roof meet (see fig. 2).

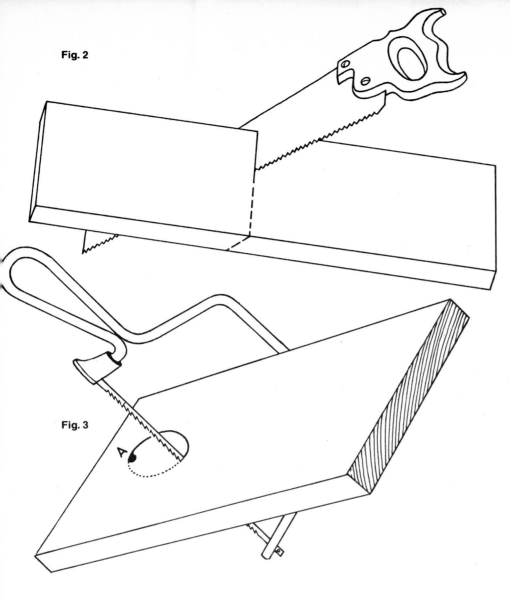

Fig. 2

Fig. 3

A

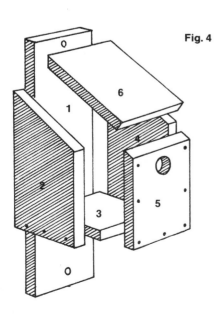

Fig. 4

1. Begin with the back.

2. Nail one side to the back. Leave some space on the top and bottom of the back, so that you can nail the box to a post or tree.

3. Nail the base onto the side and back.

4. Next, nail the second side to the base and back.

5. Now for the front. Before nailing it on, lay the roof in position, to make sure that the front does not stick up too high. If it does, you can change the position of the front to fit.

6. Nail the roof on last of all, using the strip of rubber, canvas or leather. Tack one side of the strip to the roof, and the other side to the back. Use copper tacks, if possible. This makes a hinge, so that the lid can be lifted. It is a good idea to fix little hooks or clips on both sides of the roof to hold it down. Otherwise, nail or screw down the roof. In this way, you will not be tempted to open the box too often and disturb the nesting birds.

Assembly

Cut the board in lengths as shown in fig. 1. The slopes of the two sides are formed by the one diagonal cut. The width of the base is $4\frac{1}{2}$ ins. for $\frac{3}{4}$ in.-thick wood. The exact length of the back does not matter, as long as you leave enough room top and bottom to fix the box to a post or tree.

If you tilt the saw sideways slightly (see fig. 2) when making the cut between the front and the roof (cut XX), you will neatly provide yourself with a sloping top edge for the front, and a sloping back edge for the roof. This angled cut should be made so that the front of the front piece is about $\frac{1}{4}$ in. less than the 8 ins. If this seems difficult, just make the cut straight—it does not really matter.

Entrance Hole

The entrance hole should be $1\frac{1}{8}$ in. in diameter, with its top 1 in. down from the top of the front. If you draw a circle round a 10p piece, this will give you the proper size. Cutting the hole is far easier than you might think. If you do not have a drill and bit, then use a coping saw.

First make a small hole with a bradawl or nail just inside the circle you have drawn. Take the blade off the coping saw, push it through the hole, and then fit it back onto the saw. Cut round the edge of the circle as far as you can until stopped by the frame of the saw hitting the wood. Then go back to the starting hole, unhitch the blade from the saw, and remove it from the wood. Put the blade back facing the other way, and then cut round in the other direction to make a full circle (see fig. 3). This is really quite simple, and coping saws are not very expensive.

Assembly

Next, nail the box together as shown in fig. 4. If you have used softwood and want it to last several seasons, treat it with wood preservative—on the outside only.

Making a Bird Table

For metric conversion of the measurements given here, please refer to Index.

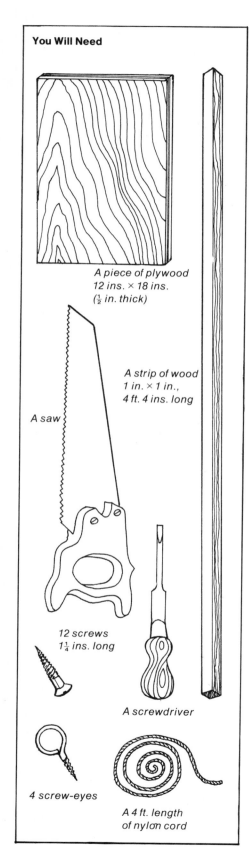

You Will Need

A piece of plywood
12 ins. × 18 ins.
(½ in. thick)

A strip of wood
1 in. × 1 in.,
4 ft. 4 ins. long

A saw

12 screws
1¼ ins. long

A screwdriver

4 screw-eyes

A 4 ft. length
of nylon cord

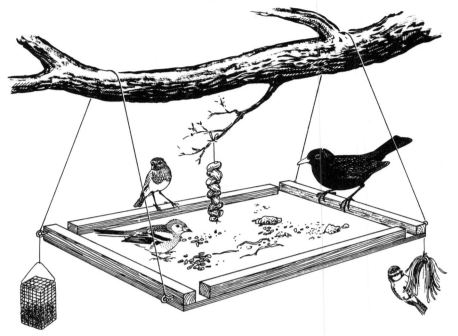

Making the Table

This bird table is very simple to make, and costs very little. All you need are a 12 ins. × 18 ins. piece of exterior quality plywood ½ in. thick, a 4 ft. 4 ins. length of 1 in. × 1 in. wood, a dozen 1¼ in. screws, and a means of supporting or hanging the table. It is important that the plywood is of exterior quality, otherwise it will quickly break up with rain or snow.

Food

What sort of food should you put on your bird table? Try kitchen scraps —bread (brown is best), cake, potatoes, chopped bacon rind, cheese, meat bones, apple cores. Seed mixtures are also a good idea, or you can buy peanuts or a coconut, or a piece of suet. In autumn, collect different sorts of berries and hang them on the table. Keep a record of which birds eat which types of food.

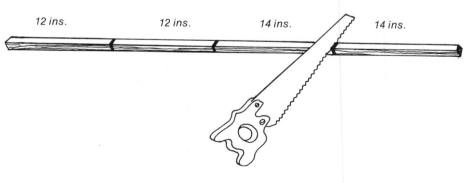

12 ins.   12 ins.   14 ins.   14 ins.

In order to prevent food from being blown off the table, and yet to allow water to drain off, cut the 1 in. × 1 in. wood into two 12 ins. lengths and two 14 ins. lengths. Fix these pieces along the top edges of the plywood,

and remember that the longest pieces of wood go along the longest sides of the plywood. This will leave a gap of about 1 in. at each corner. Water can drain off here, but the food will be protected from the wind.

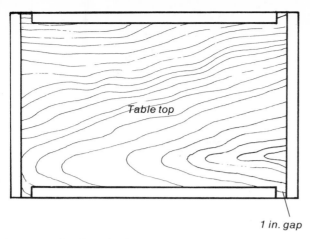

Table top

1 in. gap

This diagram shows exactly where to place the strips of wood along the edges of the plywood. You might like to make pencil marks to show you where to fix the strips of wood.

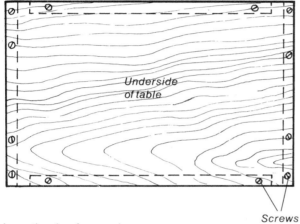

Underside of table

Screws

This diagram shows the view from underneath the bird table. It shows you where to put the screws. Make a small hole with a bradawl or a drill, before you put the screws in.

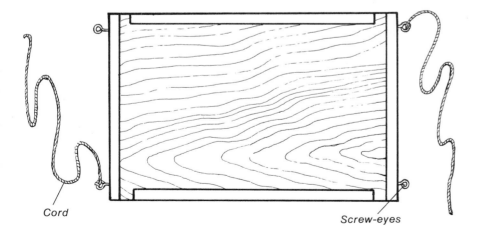

Cord

Screw-eyes

Your bird table can either be supported on a post or hung. It is simpler to hang it, provided you have a suitable tree. Just screw small brass or galvanised screw-eyes into the wooden strips at each corner of the bird table. To each of these, attach equal lengths (about 2 ft.) of terylene or nylon cord. Tie the cords to a bough.

To Make a Post Support

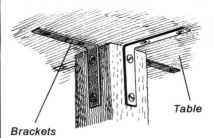

Brackets

Table

For a post, use a piece of 2 ins. × 2 ins. wood five feet high with an extra foot or so to drive into the ground. Having driven in the post, screw four metal angle brackets to the table and post, as shown above.

If you do not want to use brackets, you can form a square from four short lengths of 2 ins. × 1 in. wood, screwed through the table and to each other, fixing these to the post with a screw at each side.

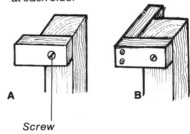

A   **B**

Screw

C   **D**

To make the square, screw the first piece of 2 ins. × 1 in. wood to the post (A). Then screw the second piece of wood to the first, as shown in (B), and screw this to the post. Do the same for the third and fourth pieces of wood as shown in (C) and (D). Screw the table to the square you have just made. Make sure it is fitted on securely.

How to Draw Birds

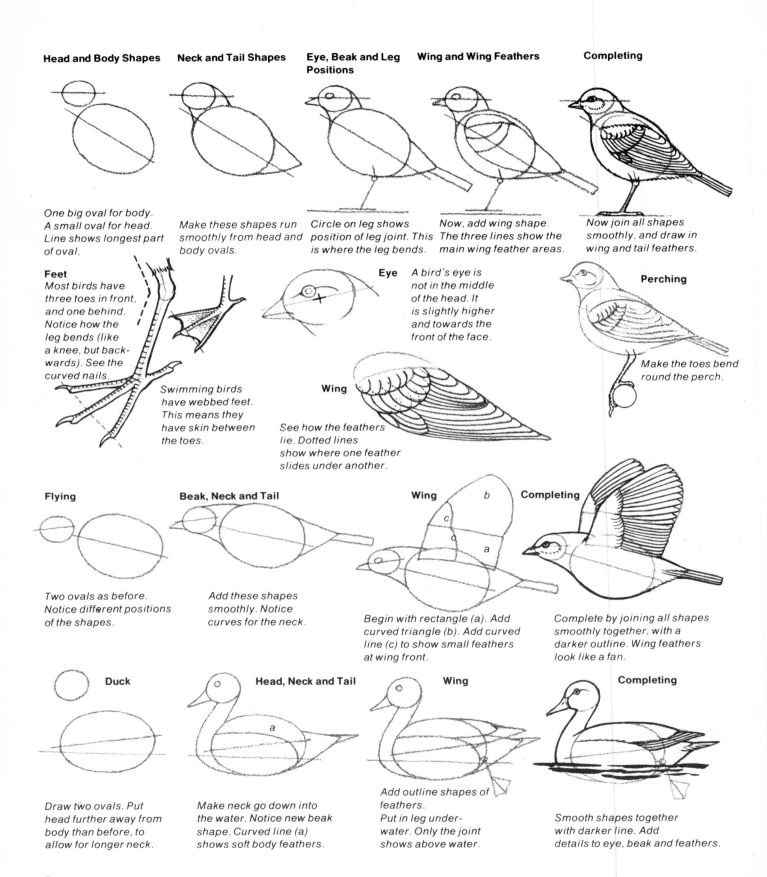

Head and Body Shapes

One big oval for body. A small oval for head. Line shows longest part of oval.

Neck and Tail Shapes

Make these shapes run smoothly from head and body ovals.

Eye, Beak and Leg Positions

Circle on leg shows position of leg joint. This is where the leg bends.

Wing and Wing Feathers

Now, add wing shape. The three lines show the main wing feather areas.

Completing

Now join all shapes smoothly, and draw in wing and tail feathers.

Feet

Most birds have three toes in front, and one behind. Notice how the leg bends (like a knee, but backwards). See the curved nails.

Swimming birds have webbed feet. This means they have skin between the toes.

Eye

A bird's eye is not in the middle of the head. It is slightly higher and towards the front of the face.

Wing

See how the feathers lie. Dotted lines show where one feather slides under another.

Perching

Make the toes bend round the perch.

Flying

Two ovals as before. Notice different positions of the shapes.

Beak, Neck and Tail

Add these shapes smoothly. Notice curves for the neck.

Wing

Begin with rectangle (a). Add curved triangle (b). Add curved line (c) to show small feathers at wing front.

Completing

Complete by joining all shapes smoothly together, with a darker outline. Wing feathers look like a fan.

Duck

Draw two ovals. Put head further away from body than before, to allow for longer neck.

Head, Neck and Tail

Make neck go down into the water. Notice new beak shape. Curved line (a) shows soft body feathers.

Wing

Add outline shapes of feathers. Put in leg under-water. Only the joint shows above water.

Completing

Smooth shapes together with darker line. Add details to eye, beak and feathers.

Names and Orders

Names
A very long time ago, when people first began calling each other by name, they had only one name each. They began to run out of names, so they used several words to describe people. The names often referred to the job they did, like 'John who beats iron into shape'. This was too much to say, so they shortened it first to 'John the Smith', and then to 'John Smith'.

Animal Names
Something like this happened with animals. First of all they were called by one name—'duck' for example. Then, when people began really to study birds, they found there were many sorts of ducks. The scholars used to write down what each bird looked like. The descriptions sometimes filled up several lines. The lists grew longer and longer the more they looked around the world.

Linnaeus
Two hundred years ago, a Swedish scientist, called Linnaeus, thought it would be easier if animals had only two names. He wanted these names to be easily understood. Not many people spoke Swedish, but at that time, all scholars spoke Latin and Greek. So Linnaeus chose these two languages to describe animals.

Two Names
The wild duck, or mallard, has a flat-bill. Linnaeus called it *Anas platyrhynchos*. *Anas* is Latin for duck, and *platyrhynchos* is Greek for flat-billed. The dog became *Canis familiaris*, which is Latin for familiar dog, or the dog which everyone knows.

Groups
There were so many animals that Linnaeus divided the animal kingdom into classes, putting animals of the same type together. He divided the classes into orders, and the orders into families. So, *Anas platyrhynchos* was placed in the family *Anatidae*. The family *Anatidae* was placed in the order *Anseriformes*, together with swans and geese, because *anser* is Latin for goose. The order *Anseriformes* was put in the class *Aves*. *Aves* is Latin for birds. There are 27 orders of birds in all.

Classification
So the wild duck fits into the animal kingdom like this:

Animal Kingdom
Class: *Aves*
Order: *Anseriformes*
Family: *Anatidae*
Genus: *Anas*
Species: *platyrhynchos*

Species
The names of species are chosen usually to say something about the animal, or say in which country it lives. Quite often, they are used to honour the person who discovered the species, or to honour a distinguished scientist.

Three Species of Duck
The genus *Anas* has three examples of how this naming works.

Anas platyrhynchos, or flat-billed duck, describes an important feature of the duck. It has a flat bill.

Anas americana, or American duck, is the name given to a bird found in America, the American wigeon, which is a kind of duck.

Anas bernieri is a duck which has been named after a Mr. Bernier.

The 27 Orders of Birds
Here is the full list of the 27 orders of birds, and some of their members:

Apterygiformes (kiwis)

Struthioniformes (ostriches)

Rheiformes (rheas)

Casuariiformes (cassowaries, emus)

Tinamiformes (tinamous)

Podicipediformes (grebes)

Gaviiformes (divers)

Sphenisciformes (penguins)

Procellariiformes (albatrosses, petrels)

Pelecaniformes (pelicans, cormorants, gannets)

Ciconiiformes (herons, storks, flamingos)

Anseriformes (swans, geese, ducks)

Falconiformes (vultures, hawks, eagles, falcons)

Galliformes (grouse, ptarmigans, quails, partridges, pheasants, turkeys)

Gruiformes (cranes, rails, bustards)

Charadriiformes (gulls, plovers, sandpipers)

Columbiformes (pigeons and doves)

Psittaciformes (parrots, cockatoos, macaws)

Cuculiformes (cuckoos)

Strigiformes (owls)

Caprimulgiformes (goatsuckers, nightjars)

Apodiformes (swifts, hummingbirds)

Trogoniformes (trogons)

Coliiformes (colies or mousebirds)

Coraciiformes (kingfishers, bee-eaters, hornbills)

Piciformes (woodpeckers)

Passeriformes (perching birds or songbirds)

Index to Pictures and Text

Metric Conversion Table		
1 in.	=	25 millimetres
3 ins.	=	76 millimetres
6 ins.	=	152 millimetres
9 ins.	=	229 millimetres
1 ft.	=	305 millimetres
1 yd.	=	914 millimetres

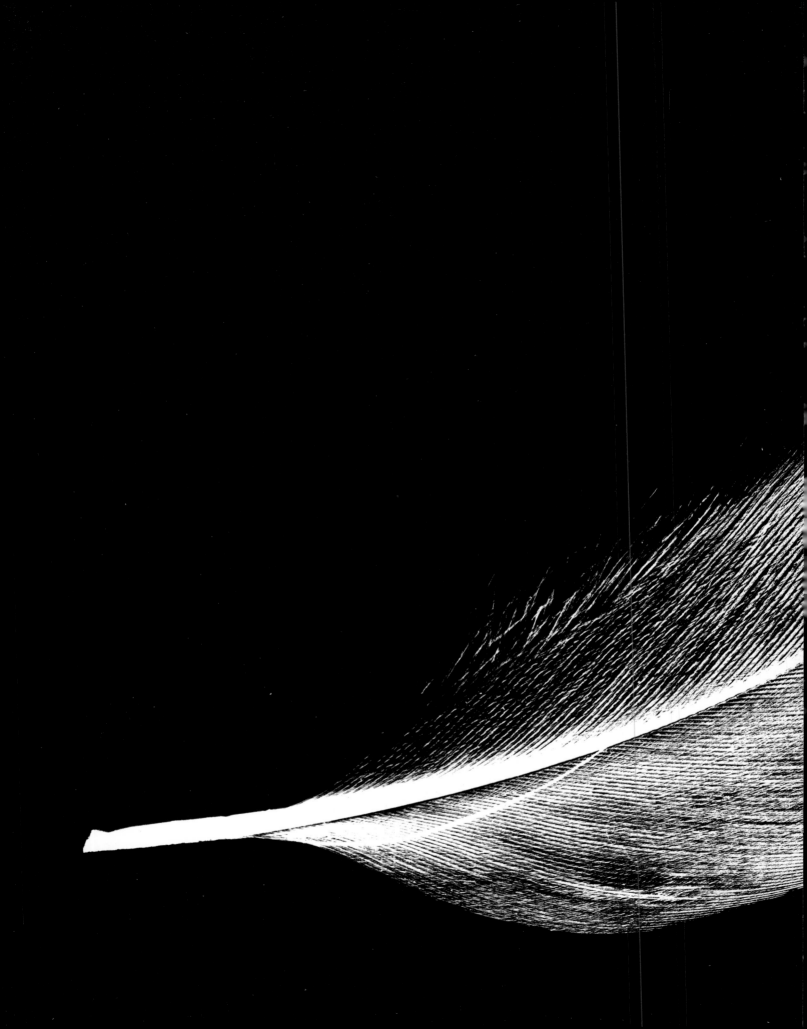